Rescuing Ourselves

A Story of Love, Healing, and Resilience Through Integrative Medicine

LARA O'NEIL, APRN, CPNP

PRAISE

"Lara O'Neil's book speaks the truth. There is no one else who can rescue us but ourselves. However, she is one of the rare healers who is willing to take on the chore of rescuing herself without the fear of failing. Rescuing ourselves is an instruction book for life. The benefits to those who do not fear taking on the self healing task are, from my experience too, what we can all accomplish when we take on the chore that life presents us with. Read her book and do not fear taking on the process of rebirthing your true self. Read and graduate into your true life with a degree from Lara."

—Bernie Siegel, MD, author of *Love, Medicine & Miracles* and *The Art of Healing*

"Lara has done it again! She has opened our eyes with her remarkable life experiences that led her to practice integrative medicine—a true gem in today's world. Through sharing her personal journey, Lara empowers readers to embrace their intuition and inner knowing with confidence and clarity. She encourages us to trust, not fear, as we seek to heal ourselves and our families by incorporating holistic medicine alongside allopathic care when needed. This beautifully written book is a testament to Lara's leap of faith, as she courageously puts herself at the forefront, sharing her wisdom and knowledge. She trusts in Spirit and her deepest consciousness, bringing her journey into the light so that you may do the same. Enjoy, and may your body, mind, and spirit reach their fullest potential in health!"

—Beverley Blass, Integrative Health

"*Rescuing Ourselves* is an illuminating story of personal and professional growth and a bold call to action to fix the ailing 'Big Medicine' machine, using the wisdom of Integrative Medicine as a guidepost. As a Psychiatric Mental Health Nurse Practitioner, a patient and a parent, reading Lara's loving words touched me to the core. She shares ways to prevent 'burn out' both personal and professional—how to humanize the increasingly productivity-oriented corporate health care system and ways to 'rescue ourselves' and improve our wellbeing by weaving the principles of integrative medicine into our practice and our daily lives. Check out Lara's prompts at the end of each chapter and her Walking Meditation and let the journey begin!"

—Ruth Goldbaum, ANP, PMHNP, MPH

"I read this book all in one sitting! It is a powerful and engaging discussion of our health care system and the problems we face as either providers and parents. Lara O'Neil, APRN has managed to pull from both her decades of experience as a health care provider, her experience as a mother, and her own deep well of both gentle and fierce passion to write a book that is inspiring for providers, and empowering for parents. It is difficult to write a book that meets the needs of these two groups of people simultaneously, but she has done it with grace and humility. She very clearly and honestly discusses the problems with the whole health care delivery system, while infusing the reader, with her hope, commitment, creativity, and validation. Any provider looking for a loving guide in dealing with some of the issues that cause us to stay up at night or burn out, give up or rebel will find this book to be essential. On the other hand if you are a parent knowing in your heart that something is wrong, and needing answers or encouragement, you have found a wise and caring guide. I am so grateful that Lara O'Neil has become the leader she has and for her loving and determined spirit."

—Miela Gruber, ND, Forest Family Medicine

"Lara O'Neil's new book, *Rescuing Ourselves: A Story of Love, Healing, and Resilience through Integrative Medicine* is part memoir, part healthcare guide, part inspiration for living one's authentic life. After experiencing the many imbalances of traditional Western medicine, O'Neil found her way as an integrative healthcare practitioner and now seeks to empower as many families as she can in their health journeys. Inspiring, well-written and a sign of the changing foundation of healthcare for the collective, *Rescuing Ourselves* is a must-read for any family in the Western medicine model who are looking for a more effective and balanced path forward."

—Dr. Heather Kristian Strang, Mpsy.D, author of *Love Letters From Mary Magdalene: The Untold Tale of Her Life, Love & Legacy*

Rescuing Ourselves: A Story of Love, Healing, and Resilience through Integrative Medicine
By Lara O'Neil, APRN, CPNP

Published by Flower of Life Press
www.floweroflifepress.com

Flower of Life Press books may be ordered through booksellers or by contacting:
support@floweroflifepress.com

Cover and Interior design: Astara Jane Ashley

Library of Congress Control Number: Available upon request.

ISBN: 979-8-9909775-6-3

Dedication

To my incredible mother, who sadly passed away a few months before this book went to publication. She was one of my biggest cheerleaders to complete this project and share my message, even in my own doubts. In her honor and to continue her legacy, I hope to impart seeds of change, hope, inspiration, and, most of all, love.

Table of Contents

PREFACE

There was a time in my life when I felt like I had a split personality. Not full-blown Sybil stuff, but troublesome, nonetheless. I was working in a traditional pediatric office and seeing patients every 10-15 minutes, working in a model of care where "wellness visits" were focused primarily on vaccinations, and symptoms of illness were mostly treated with medications. These aspects of pediatric care are undeniably important, but individuality often took the backseat, and investigating root causes was a rarity due to time constraints.

The consideration of culture, religion, values, or individual choice was often overlooked. Children seemed to be growing sicker, and chronic diseases were on the rise. I loved what I did, but I longed to give more, help more, and make a bigger difference. Quantity rather than quality of care was emphasized, and the office culture was tainted by conformity and toxicity. I dreamed of finding another job in integrative medicine where I could practice the way that I wanted to, the way that my heart yearned to. Many patients sought me out, longing for this kind of care, and I did my best within the constraints of my role. These moments brought me immense satisfaction, especially when I knew I'd made a positive difference.

Even though I wasn't satisfied with my career, I was a single mom with three young children and needed the security of a good income and benefits. I had worked hard and had a lot of schooling to get where I was. I longed for someone to offer me my dream job, but years went by, and, well, that never happened.

Outside of work, I found solace through meditation, yoga classes, and retreats. I sought care from integrative healers for myself and my children, choosing natural therapies when possible. I took classes, seminars, and workshops and read everything I could about integrative medicine, natural remedies, and holistic health. During these times, I was happy and content. Yet, when I returned to work, I felt miserable, almost like an imposter.

I knew this separation was diminishing my effectiveness in both areas of life. I became increasingly miserable, stressed, and exhausted. I became short-tempered with my children and disappointed in myself.

The final straw came in a moment I remember very vividly. During a lunchtime staff meeting, I was belabored for running twenty minutes late while another patient was waiting. This happened all the time with the other doctors, not just me, but for some reason, that day it became a long topic of conversation where I was vilified. I sat there silently, feeling a pit in my stomach. I was an excellent employee who had been with the practice for nine years and was well-liked by the patients. My lateness resulted from the inadequate 15-minute slots allotted for each patient, and I was trying to give the best care possible within these constraints.

The next morning, I cried the entire twenty-minute drive to work. It wasn't just about what had transpired at the staff meeting but the culmination of events throughout my career. At that moment, I had an epiphany—I knew, from the bottom of my soul, that I could no longer continue down this path. What the Hell had I been thinking?

My work had become soul-crushing. I wanted to help children and their families, but how could I do that if I couldn't even help myself? I needed to take a leap of faith, follow my heart and desires, leave my job, and venture out on my own. Don't get me wrong, it was terrifying. I doubted myself, and I was sick with fear about being able to support myself and my children financially. I grieved the families and patients I would be leaving behind. I had many sleepless nights. Yet, despite all the apprehension, I knew, from a profound place, that I was making the right decision. I was being called to find my purpose in soul-driven work. It was my divine feminine reclamation. So, I began the process of alchemizing the two worlds I was living in.

This is my story. I hope it inspires you. I hope it is thought-provoking. Within these pages, I share the journey from my childhood, traversing the hopes, challenges, dreams, and reflections on the future of our struggling healthcare system.

INTRODUCTION

"Integrative Medicine is the practice of medicine that reaffirms the importance of the relationship between practitioner and patient, focuses on the whole person, is informed by evidence, and makes use of all appropriate therapeutic approaches, healthcare professionals, and disciplines to achieve optimal health and healing."

~The Consortium of Academic Health Centers for Integrative Medicine

Imagine you and I sitting across from one another in a coffee shop. You have your latte, and I will share the story of my evolution as a healthcare provider and...well, as a person. And I would love to hear your story! We're just two moms being real.

I'm not your average stiff white-coat healthcare provider. I understand the struggles and frustrations you have with the healthcare industry. I have them as well. I'm going to be vulnerable and honest with you. I think you will relate to many of my stories in one way or another. In a way that is meaningful to you. I would love to know what has meaning for you.

Have you ever experienced that moment when you look at your child, and the sheer cuteness in that little face makes you want to smother them in a thousand kisses? Your heart overflows with love for this little one, and you're certain you'd jump in front of a train for them. But then, on the flip side, after they've asked you for a snack and spilled it all over the floor for the umpteenth time, the urge to run and scream out of the house like a lunatic takes over. You find yourself daydreaming about checking into a hotel for a week, where you can sleep whenever you want, use the bathroom in peace, eat on your own schedule, watch TV, or read a book without anyone clamoring for your attention. You know that feeling, right? Experiencing both of these emotions simultaneously.

Well, I promise you, you are not crazy. You do not have multiple personalities, even though it feels like it. Trust me, I know! It is normal. You are allowed to feel all the feelings—and it doesn't make you a bad mom. It doesn't make you a bad person. And it doesn't make you love and care for your children any less. It simply makes you human. In fact, it makes you a great mom! And it is entirely legitimate to have a complex and multidimensional emotional experience. It is a beautiful thing. Life is not just "either/or." It actually is "both/and." It makes us the wise, interesting, juicy, deep, and incredible people we are.

So, what's my point about this dramatic description? For me, finding integrative medicine has some parallels to balancing the challenges of parenthood. It doesn't have to be one or the other. It's both. Two opposing thoughts working towards a unified truth. It offers a solution to those moments of inner conflict, exhaustion, and a sense of inauthenticity. It's about embracing the "best of both worlds." Integrative medicine has enabled me to integrate my education, experience, love of science, and desire to help people recover from diseases and maintain good health, all while honoring my own sovereignty and unwavering belief in natural, holistic healing. This approach allows me to provide heart-centered and intuitive care, facilitating genuine assistance to others and my own self-care.

There is a better way for our failing healthcare system. How do I know this? I have been in pediatric healthcare for over thirty years. I have worked in many settings within the traditional Western medical model. Nearly ten years ago, when I was literally busting at the seams and couldn't take it anymore, I left and started my own integrative healthcare practice. It saved me and allowed me to continue a career in the healthcare industry while avoiding complete burnout.

This personal transformation story is imbued with a vision for a new healthcare paradigm for children and their families, told through the lens of a Renegade Pediatric Nurse Practitioner. Yep, that's me.

Why I Wrote this Book

There are two reasons why I decided to write this book and share my message. First, my current practice has a long waiting list of patients who want to see us for the care of their children. I wish I could see them all, but as a small practice, we can only see a certain number of patients each day and provide primary care to a limited number of families each year to maintain the quality care we're dedicated to offering. Second, throughout the years, I have had several providers reach out, expressing interest in transitioning to integrative healthcare, but they struggle to figure out how to branch out of conventional medicine. Conventional medicine often fails to provide meaningful solutions to our many health issues. Parents are seeking healthcare providers they can trust, while healthcare providers are aiming to practice in a more meaningful way. I want to show you how we can meet that goal.

If you are a parent, especially a parent who's also a healthcare provider, this book is for you! After all, all moms, by vocation or nature, are inherently healthcare providers. I love empowering mothers to care for their children and themselves. We are all overwhelmed and need a sense of community, support, and a feeling that we have each other's back.

I'm here to share what I have learned and to empower you. You'll find anecdotal stories, patient stories, and some very personal and vulnerable moments to help you better understand this journey. I want you to know that I have faced my own challenges and persevered. At the end of the chapters, I have included journal prompts to encourage reflection and integration of what you've read into something meaningful for you.

My hope is for change. A lot of people want it. I know we can do it. A lot of parents are asking for it. Many healthcare providers want to offer it. I hope to reach more people through this book that I otherwise couldn't reach in my small corner of the world. I see myself as a warrior, and if you're reading this, you're a warrior, too—one with humility, modesty, skill, and grit.

If you are a healthcare provider who wants to provide care in a better way and are frustrated by the current healthcare system, we need you, and I have faith in you! If you are a parent and want healthcare for your child with your family's best interest at heart, then you can absolutely have that! I wrote this with you in mind. We need change. We deserve better. Let's do this together.

xo, Lara

CHAPTER 1

FORMATIVE EXPERIENCES: SETTING THE STAGE

"I believe the children are our future, teach them well and let them lead the way, show them all the beauty they possess inside."

-Lyrics from the song "The Greatest Love of All" by Linda Creed (1977)

Picture a two-year-old me, squatted in the dirt, dutifully scooping soil into my mouth. I am next to my mother, who is planting in her small garden plot behind our apartment building in Waltham, MA. It was a common occurrence, and Farmer Joe would casually stroll by, saying, "They say you eat a pound of dirt before you die. Well, I guess Lara is just getting all of hers now." Since my mom was always playing in it, I must have assumed that there was goodness in there (I would make Dr. Maya Shetreat-Klein—author of The Dirt Cure—proud).

I have wondered if my little body innately knew that it needed something to nourish it, and as a dirt-eating-toddler, I was drawn to the earth's soil to supply it. I was getting some natural nutrients and probiotics, and this was 1972 before they flooded the supplement market. I know that may sound odd to some people, but I am always thinking about these things, trying to understand them on a deeper level. It's just the way I have always been.

I am sharing the following stories with you to explore the building blocks that shaped my perspective on health and led me into the world of integrative medicine. Also, I want to let you know that you are not alone in experiencing healthcare challenges and disappointments. I think at least some of these stories will resonate with you in one form or another.

Early Health Struggles

According to my mother, I cried a lot as an infant and was diagnosed with colic. I was a picky eater as a young child, and for some time, apparently, I only ate hamburger meat and applesauce. A little later in my childhood, I developed eczema.

My mother was a bit of a "crunchy granola type." She introduced me to muscle testing, also known as kinesiology, through the reverent Dr. Sidney Baker, whom some lovingly refer to as the father of integrative medicine—we were lucky enough to live a few blocks away from him at the time. She told him I was pale and had eczema and dark circles under my eyes, and he explained how my symptoms could be related to food sensitivities. I remember standing in our kitchen with my mother when I was ten. She instructed me to hold out my arm and resist her from pushing it downwards to establish my strength. Then she put small amounts of different foods in my mouth, and we repeated the muscle test to ensure I maintained the same strength I had established. We tried various foods, and I maintained my arm strength for most of them. The pivotal moment came when I put a small amount of wheat bread into my mouth. My arm succumbed to the pressure and went much lower than it had previously. We repeated it a few times, and much to my dismay, it continued to do the same thing. I couldn't believe it. And I tried really hard to hold my arm stronger, trust me! Therefore, she thought wheat could be causing my eczema. I thought she was a nut job, but I was intrigued. Clearly, my body did not respond well to it. So, I went on a wheat-free diet, and the eczema cleared up quickly. True story.

It may have seemed strange, but this experience was my first step into the holistic health world, where the focus was on understanding the wisdom of the body, root causes, and not just symptoms. Since then, I have had the honor and privilege of conversing with the esteemed Dr. Baker. His accomplishments are nothing short of awe-inspiring. I am so grateful for his work and for paving the way for integrative practitioners like myself, even before it was "trendy" and more accepted.

Growing Up in a Gluten-Unfriendly World

In the 80s, it was not easy to eat a wheat-free diet. The bread was rock hard and tasted like brick and earth. The pasta fell apart. The wheat-free flours made for very disappointing cookies and baked goods. This was long before the gluten-free fad of today, and very little could be found. I felt weird and self-conscious because none of my other friends had food restrictions, and feeling any weirder and more self-conscious is not exactly what a pre-teen hopes for. Things have changed a lot over the last several decades, and now it is more common than not to have food sensitivities. Of course, the reasons for this are another topic of conversation, albeit an important one. But since the market meets demand, it is now flooded with many different allergy-free options.

In my later teen years, it was usual that my friends would all want to go out for pizza. After all, we lived in New Haven, CT, which is known for having the best pizza in the country! (Hint: Pepe's and Sally's). I wanted to be a part of this, so I either wouldn't eat anything or would just order fries or salad. But one time, my friend Chris told me that when he ate cheese, he would often feel nauseous and get an upset stomach. So, we decided to share the pizza. I would eat the cheese on the top, and he would eat the bread on the bottom. Brilliant! It was fun to have a "weird food partner" initially, but it quickly got old. The just eating melted greasy cheese part, that is. So, one time, for no apparent reason, I thought, "Screw this! My mom is crazy and probably making this wheat allergy thing up. I'm just going to eat this pizza and enjoy myself!" So, I ate the pizza, and I did enjoy myself. I did not have any apparent symptoms or side effects and felt vindicated! You know...that adolescent rebellious feeling of "See, my mom was wrong all along, and I knew it!" I proceeded to eat gluten without acknowledging that it could have been causing my eczema flare-ups for the next seventeen years.

Disillusioned with Conventional Medicine

As for my father, a scientist and pharmacology professor at Yale, this type of "voodoo" medicine my mother embraced wasn't quite up his alley. He decided I needed to see a conventional doctor and brought me to a Yale allergy clinic for blood testing. I remember very well when the doctor came out to give us the results, quickly said, "Everything is normal," and then walked away. He didn't express interest in what we have tried, how we could address the eczema, or why we did the blood test in the first place. The test showed that I had no allergies, and that was that. In this case, his evidence-based standard protocol blood tests were just downright missing the boat. But it took me a while to figure that out.

In my early teens, I developed a circular rash on my lower leg that lasted for months. Again, my father wanted me to see a Yale dermatologist. She diagnosed it with ringworm and prescribed an antifungal cream, but it did not clear up the rash in the least bit. Eventually, it just resolved on its own. Unfortunately, that esteemed Yale dermatologist misdiagnosed me. That was the pattern of my eczema. Depending on what was happening in my life, it would come and go and move between different parts of my body.

Legacy of Health Struggles

My mother has also been a bit of a medical mystery. When I was 15, she started developing concerning health symptoms, but nobody could figure out why. It took the medical community fifteen years to finally diagnose her with Primary Progressive Multiple Sclerosis (MS), which is a little different than the more common Relapsing and Remitting MS. For years, she went to specialist after specialist, and every specialist believed it was something they specialized in. And every specialist ordered the tests that those particular specialists ordered. The infectious doctor thought it was Lyme disease, the GI doctor thought it was a parasite, and the Rheumatologist thought it was Homocystinuria. She was treated with all the different medications for each of these diseases and never made any improvements. In fact, she continued to get worse.

When I was older, my mother's Rheumatologist told her that I should also see a doctor and check for Homocystinuria since it could be genetic. And if so, I should not be on birth control (which I already had been for several years)—it could affect my fertility and reduce my chances of getting pregnant (which I happened to be at the time). I asked my Midwife to order the bloodwork, and the homocysteine results came back slightly elevated. She referred me to a Hematologist and gave me a pretty good scare. But the Hematologist didn't want to see me because I was pregnant.

And round and round we go. So, I never got any answers or guidance and was left worrying about it for many months. It turned out that my mother never had Homocystinuria after all.

Years later, I figured out on my own that this slight elevation in my homocysteine at the time of that blood draw, as well as hers, was most likely because our family had a genetic variation called Methylenetetrahydrofolate reductase (MTHFR).

My maternal Aunt has also experienced autoimmune problems and bouts of depression. Doctors have tried putting her on many different types of medications, all of which she has had bad reactions to. To this day, she is in continuous pain from her Rheumatoid Arthritis, regular medicine has been unable to help her, and traditional doctors continue to get dismissive and frustrated by her inability to tolerate their recommended treatments.

My Grandmother's Health Odyssey

My grandmother suffered from severe bouts of eczema that covered her body for most of her adult life. Her skin would be red, cracked, inflamed, and painful when she had her flares. Her doctors put her on steroid bursts multiple times throughout the years. When that stopped working, they started prescribing methotrexate, which is a drug used for conditions like cancer, rheumatoid arthritis, and psoriasis for immunosuppression. Nobody ever talked to her about other ways to treat her eczema except to stop using products that had fragrance in them. My children, my mother, myself, and my cousin are all very sensitive to gluten, and it is highly possible that if she tried a gluten-free diet, her eczema would have improved substantially as it did for me. But of course, we will never know. She was of the generation that "Doctor knows best." So, when I spoke to her about it, it wasn't even in the realm of possibilities. Instead, I believe that all the medications she was prescribed to treat it ultimately killed her.

After years of being repeatedly put on this toxic drug when her eczema flared, her Rheumatologist finally said that she absolutely could not be on methotrexate anymore, that it would not be safe for her. But then, when she had another bad flare and went to a dermatologist, he prescribed it for her again. Even though she was 80, she was otherwise very healthy, vibrant, and full of life. One day, seemingly unexplained, she appeared a little more disoriented to my aunt, so she brought her to the doctor to be evaluated.

She had a very low pulse oximetry reading, so she was admitted to the hospital. They discovered that she had severe lung damage (a potential side effect of methotrexate) and that her "lungs were like crushed glass." She died suddenly and unexpectedly a few weeks later from pulmonary fibrosis. It was devastating. I loved her deeply, and she was always an important part of my life since I was young. We will never know for sure, but I truly believe that that outcome could have been very different if she had better healthcare all along.

Health Issues Revisited and Frustrations

Throughout my adult life, the eczema would flare up, get better, and continue this cycle of reoccurrence. In hindsight, it would often be worse at times of increased stress, like starting nursing school, demanding jobs, pregnancies, lack of sleep as a new mom, and even when my marriage began to fall apart.

In my mid-20s, I discovered a small lump under the inside of my nose, so I went to a family physician. He poked around at it with a stern face and barely said anything except that it was concerning and that I needed an MRI. I went for the imaging a few weeks later, the soonest I could schedule it. I was already nervous because the doctor made it seem serious but didn't give me any other guidance, and I already had a few weeks to worry about it. The imaging technician was distant and cold. He instructed me to lay face down, came over and gruffly adjusted my head, then barked at me not to move through the whole session and quickly walked into the other room to run the machine. When he adjusted my head, he actually lifted it up ever so slightly so my face was not resting in the face cradle; therefore, I had to use my neck muscles to hold it up. After a few minutes, my neck became really uncomfortable, slowly increasing until it became painful. He did not give me any direction on how long it would take, and it seemed to be taking forever, but I was scared to move even a hairline because of his abrasive instructions. Finally, he came out and told me I could leave. I couldn't get out of there fast enough! My neck hurt for several days after that.

My doctor called me a few days later and said they didn't know what it was, but it could be a "problem," and I needed to see a specialist. Interestingly, it was gone before I could even get in with the specialist! It was winter now, and it was the fall season when I first discovered it. Fast forward several years later, I discovered a clear pattern of it swelling up around the time I experienced fall allergy symptoms, and then it would resolve. The doctor never asked any questions or explored any possibilities of what could be causing it. He only considered the physical symptom of the small lump and the physical location. All that worrying, physical pain, and medical bills possibly could have been avoided, or at least reduced, if he had taken more time with me. And it was a very straightforward problem.

A few years later, after my first pregnancy, I had a severe eczema flare-up on my hands that looked like a second-degree burn. This was especially hard since I worked as a nurse in the hospital and was constantly using my hands for patient care and frequent handwashing. I saw a Dermatologist, who prescribed steroid cream and sent me on my way. It would get a little better, but then it would continue to flare up and never fully resolve. I went back to the Dermatologist, who then prescribed a psoriasis treatment. This sloughed off the first layer of my skin like a reptile, and the eczema bubbled up again as the skin healed. This vicious cycle repeated several times until I decided not to do that anymore. For-crying-out-loud!

Frustrated that I wasn't getting any help, I decided to see an Allergist. They wanted to give me a more potent prescription steroid cream but still didn't address what was causing it in the first place. I asked if I could do allergy testing because I wanted more answers, not just more creams. He "snarfed" it off and said that if I were allergic to something, it would be all over my body, not just my hands. I persisted in my request, so he begrudgingly succumbed to the allergy testing. The results showed that I was highly allergic to fragrance (which was in the creams I was using on my hands to try to help), latex (in the gloves I was wearing while working in the hospital), formaldehyde (which is in an alarming amount of beauty industry products as a preservative. Yup, the same one used to embalm dead bodies…), and a substance in rubber that made it pliable (which was in things like IV tubing and IV fluid bags that I was handling daily). I dutifully went home, scoured the list of ingredients, and got rid of bags and bags of products I was using on myself, in my home, and for my baby. I replaced everything with natural, fragrance-free, and hypoallergenic products. The financial implications were hard to swallow at first since I also had to replace everything, but now I could never go back to using those products again.

The eczema did clear up on my hands. I am so grateful I got those toxins out for myself and my child. And my skin had a stellar few years. If I hadn't pressed for an explanation, the doctors would have been happy to keep prescribing stronger and more potent steroid creams without any interest in investigating why I might even have these issues in the first place.

Revisiting Old Symptoms

A few years later, when I was pregnant again with the twins, I developed a rash around my nose and mouth. I mentioned it to my mother as we talked on the phone, and she said, "Well, you know, dear, it sounds like what you had as a child, and wheat caused it." I had forgotten about that chapter in my life, so I didn't think that could be it. And I certainly didn't want it to be that. But the rash was quite bothersome, and I knew by then that going to the doctor would be futile. So, I decided to try going on a gluten-free diet, even though giving up that Oreo ice cream was devastating! I was pregnant and starving! But the rash cleared up. If I made tiny mistakes, like exposures from dressings, marinades, or even one little Starburst, the rash would come roaring back. My theory is that the extra physiological demand of the pregnancy on my body made it so that I couldn't process gluten well again, which was never good for me in the first place.

Seeds of Service

You may see a pattern here. Before my advanced practice career, I had experienced medical doctors and specialists. No one had any answers or helpful guidance, and I was repeatedly disappointed and perpetually let down by the medical system. I'm just lucky that it wasn't anything more serious for me. But unfortunately, many people have similar stories. And many of them are significantly worse.

A seed was being planted. I wanted to become a better provider, one that would allow people to have a very different type of experience with the healthcare system.

It's important to clarify that I greatly respect healthcare providers and medical doctors, as they are my colleagues. They possess intelligence, dedication, and a genuine passion for helping people and are committed to their mission. However, the broader healthcare industry grapples with deep-rooted limiting issues driven by profit and a one-size-fits-all algorithm. This, in turn, has led to a trend of over-medicalization stemming from a lack of allotted time as well as a fear of liability. Many of these dedicated healthcare professionals work in a system they may not fully comprehend, where insurance companies and pharmaceutical corporations wield excessive power and influence, prioritizing financial gains over patients' well-being. This system leads to huge gaps, disappointments, and voids that people may feel when seeking healthcare for themselves or their loved ones.

Journal Prompt

What experiences or moments in your younger years have shaped you significantly? Do you have similar stories in healthcare or any other industry, even from a person or group of people, where you were let down or didn't feel like you fit in? Has it made you do things differently now? Or have hopes to do things differently in the future?

You might have several things to say here or just one defining moment. It can be minor or significant, or anything in between. It doesn't matter; whatever comes up is perfect.

CHAPTER 2

The Preparation: Tales from an Insider

"Everybody's searching for a hero, people need someone to look up to. I never found anyone to fulfill my needs, a lonely place to be, and so I learned to depend on me."

-Lyrics from the song "The Greatest Love of All"
by Linda Creed (1977)

When I was in high school, I was interested in becoming either a veterinarian or an OB/GYN doctor. Then, in my first year at college, I considered social services, but that was short-lived. I enrolled in some courses in Social Work and Psychology. I have always found human psychology to be fascinating and was drawn to work in the areas of human services. But it still didn't give me exactly what I was looking for. It wasn't until after talking with a friend about nursing school that my passion was ignited. I was fascinated with science, anatomy, and how the human body works, coupled with serving and helping others. In healthcare, interpersonal skills and scientific knowledge are a complex balance. I wanted to do better, give more, and make a difference in people's lives.

When I first considered Nursing school, I felt inspired and excited. The fusion of science and care-giving clicked for me. So, I transferred to the School of Nursing at the University of Vermont, where I fell in love with pediatrics and the newborn nursery. Nursing's holistic approach, focusing not just on disease and illness but on the whole person and the systems that influence health, resonated with my values. At one point, I thought I might return to school to become a Nurse Midwife.

However, it wasn't until I worked as a Registered Nurse in the newborn nursery in Minneapolis that my true calling became clear. During this time, Pediatric Nurse Practitioners would come into the nursery for the newborn exams. Although I didn't know much about the profession, they graciously taught me how to examine a newborn and what to look for. Their dedication to caring for infants deeply impressed me. I started conversations with them about their careers and what they did for children and families. It was then that I realized that this was exactly what I wanted to do. I was hooked and knew I had found my true path.

From Graduate School to Pediatric Practice

Wide-eyed and bushy-tailed, I completed graduate school and passed my boards to be a Certified Pediatric Nurse Practitioner. I was excited to help children and their families in a new way. I wanted families to have positive healthcare experiences and feel the value of having a trusted pediatrician as part of their team.

My career led me to the St. Paul, Minnesota school system, where I worked for a few years. After having the twins, and now with three young children, we decided to move back to Connecticut to be close to family. I briefly worked part-time in a hospital's newborn nursery before transitioning to a hustling and bustling pediatric primary care office.

My boss, the head pediatrician, was a brilliant man for whom I had immense respect. I am eternally grateful for the almost ten years I was his employee and the invaluable lessons I learned from him. He had a wealth of knowledge and experience in pediatrics and was adored by many of our families. Within a minute or two of seeing a patient, he would know if it was a particularly concerning health problem. And whether it was or wasn't, he would be a calming and reassuring presence. He was kind, listened, soft-spoken, gentle, and accepting of choice, yet authoritarian when necessary. Though never rushing to over-medicalize or intervene, he would certainly do so when warranted. Having been trained in traditional Western medicine in the late 60s and 70s, he was "old school," and that was exactly how he practiced. He valued clinical skills and physical exams and scoffed at the overuse of diagnostic interventions and expensive pharmaceuticals. He recognized the importance of nurse practitioners and had them working with him from the early days, even before it became commonplace. Pharmaceutical representatives with fancy suits and glossy marketing materials were promptly kicked out of his office, and he refused their offers for free fancy dinners as they touted the magic of their products backed by the research that was funded by, well...them. Most importantly, he believed in the long-term relationship between pediatricians and patients and felt that most things could be addressed in primary care without needing specialists. It was not uncommon to have his former patients bring their own children to him for care, a practice I admired and looked forward to continuing in my own career.

After a few months of working at the primary care office, I approached my boss for feedback on my performance. I initiated this conversation because I was anxious to know if he felt I was doing a good job and if the patients were satisfied with their care. To my surprise, he took out a piece of paper and started jotting down the numbers of how many patients he expected me to see in increasing increments over the next few months. I was taken aback that our discussion was about quantity rather than quality. Nevertheless, I ultimately agreed to see more patients, which unfortunately meant less time with each individual.

Setting Up for Burn-Out

My boss wasn't motivated by greed or narrow-mindedness. However, to make his practice profitable within the health insurance model, his providers needed to see a large volume of patients. This approach, although profitable, set us up for a cookie-cutter model of care that left very little room to identify the root causes of illness or offer transformative education. It also created provider burnout and reduced the ability to provide quality care. This business model was the reality within which we all had to operate.

And to add to the stress, when we became ill while working, we knew that we would still be expected to come to work. I felt overwhelming guilt on the rare occasions when I had to call in sick for myself or my children. Schedules were so jam-packed with patients that the other providers couldn't cover last minute or even have time to reach the families coming in to reschedule. It was ironic that those responsible for caring for the patients weren't permitted to take care of themselves, as it would create too much stress on the busy schedules of other providers, let alone the spread of disease. I remember how sheepish I felt one day while seeing a child whose mother was going through chemotherapy, therefore immunocompromised, while I was battling a severe cough. Or when I had to carry my crying children to work and lay them on the floor of my office due to fever, vomiting, or, incredibly, a broken bone—all instead of caring for them at home in their beds where they belonged.

If the clinic was such an unsupported environment for the health and well-being of the providers, how could it support the patients?

The traditional healthcare industry's model generally lacks significant support for patients as well as employees. Conversations about burnout in physicians and healthcare providers, along with statistics about suicide rates, are not uncommon. Nurses often work in challenging conditions, including unsafe patient-staff ratios, unreasonably long hours, overtime due to staff shortages, and lack of respect from physicians.

Looking for Answers in the Wrong Places

There were multiple times during this part of my career when I had concerns about a patient and also had doubts about how to best help them. I vividly remember seeing a school-aged child with cold symptoms in my first year at the pediatric office. She had a runny nose and a mild cough for a few days, and her mom brought her in for evaluation. Her physical exam was normal, and she was an otherwise healthy child. I diagnosed her with an upper respiratory infection (URI), which is basically a fancy word for a cold, and sent them home. The following week, she returned to the office because she had developed a worsening cough and a fever. This time, she saw my colleague, who was an MD. Her lungs were still clear, but because of the history of her getting worse, she sent them for an X-ray, which identified pneumonia, and she was started on antibiotics. The mother became angry and said she never wanted to see an APRN again and would only see an MD from now on. My colleague, who saw her for the second visit, told me that she would not have done anything differently than I had done if she had seen her the week prior. And I knew that if I were the provider seeing the child the second time, but now with worsening symptoms, then I would order the X-ray as well. Unfortunately, the doctor didn't explain that to the mother, and it was labeled in her chart as "MD ONLY."

I felt shame that the mother thought that I did not provide good care to her child, and I felt betrayed that my colleagues did not support me. But as I reflect now, even though it was many years ago, I realize that if I had the integrative tools that I have now to offer better suggestions around how to support a child through an illness, even mild ones, and to provide natural treatments, then the outcome potentially could have been much better for everyone involved. But since there is no prescription medication for a common cold, and the standard over-the-counter medications provide only temporary symptom relief at best, I wasn't able to educate and support the mom to help her feel empowered to take care of her child at home, to potentially avoid a second visit to the doctor's office, or to feel that her pediatrician was taking good care of her child.

On another occasion, I saw a teenage girl who was having a lot of problems with her menstrual cycle, and her mom brought her to the office for help. She also sought care from a functional medicine doctor and asked if I would collaborate with him. I had never heard of functional medicine but was interested in hearing about the approach, as I always loved to learn new things. Our office standard of care would be to put her on birth control pills to regulate her cycles in the hopes that it would reduce the problems that she was experiencing. The conversation with her functional medicine doctor was about hormones and stress and the testing he was doing for her that would give insight into how to best support her. I was instantly intrigued. This approach made a whole lot more sense to me than to put a young teenage girl who was not yet sexually active on synthetic hormones that did not come without potential side effects.

In 2011, the American Academy of Pediatrics (AAP) recommended that all children between the ages of 10-11 should be screened for cholesterol levels. This was in response to the NHLBI (National Heart, Lung, and Blood Institute) guidelines initiated because of the alarming increase in obesity in our children. My office dutifully purchased a lipids screening test kit that could be used right in the office with immediate results. We started testing every 11-year-old who came in for a physical regardless of any risk factors. Because of my concern that we didn't have any plan regarding education or treatment options, I brought it up with my boss. I asked him what we would do if a child had elevated lipids, and his answer was, "Put him on a statin, I guess." I found this answer to be alarming for many reasons. A statin drug does not come without the possibility of significant side effects, let alone that this completely ignores the question of why such a young child would have elevated lipids. Education and some changes in lifestyle at a young age could help prevent a whole litany of other issues that would come later in life. But this would take time and would not necessarily be easy. And neither of those factors works well in our current healthcare paradigm of just treating the symptom with medication and ignoring root causes.

In nursing school, I was taught to speak with the doctors if I didn't have the answer. But all too often, the answers I would get would not be what I was looking for or no different than the options I had already considered. The recommendation would often just be to put them on a medication or a different medication than what they were already on. Still, I knew that wasn't getting at the root problem or providing the answers the parent was looking for. Quickly, I realized that I was looking for answers in the wrong places. Don't get me wrong, these doctors were very smart, good doctors. They knew a tremendous amount about disease. They would swiftly, purposefully, and effectively respond to acute and emergency situations. But their training and education didn't teach them what I was looking for—not for these types of situations. I knew I needed to find answers elsewhere.

Seeing through the Bu*$%it

In February 2013, we had a severe winter storm that caused power outages, which forced us to close the office for two days. I remember very well my conversation with my boss when we were back in the office. We were remarking that it was surprising that the phones weren't as crazy as we expected since we had been closed the previous two days. He told me privately, "The problem is that now all the patients know that they don't need to come in every time they get sick, that they will just get better in a few days if they stay home." We laughed it off, but that really struck me, and I reflect on it to this day.

In Dr. Robert Mendelsohn's acclaimed and controversial book *How to Raise a Healthy Child, In Spite of Your Doctor,* he talks about not going to your pediatrician when your kid is sick. The man had some valid points, even though one could say he was talking himself out of a career! He was a brilliant doctor, and I admire his spirit and willingness to be a well-known maverick in the medical profession. But he knew nothing about integrative medicine and what it could offer. Neither did my boss.

Reaching the Point of No Return

Patient after patient, day after day, year after year, I found myself practicing in a way that I didn't truly believe was beneficial. I found myself increasingly disinterested. Unfortunately, it was the nature of the job and the way the office was run. During wellness exams, there just wasn't enough time to delve into crucial aspects like nutrition, emotional health, or root causes of issues. Ironically, I was relieved and grateful when parents didn't have many questions, and the child was perfectly healthy, as it allowed me to do the exams quickly without falling behind or getting stressed. Contrarily, prescribing medications for symptoms during acute illnesses or consult appointments was much easier and faster than doing the harder and more nuanced work of delving into root causes, providing valuable education, and answering parents' questions.

Consequently, I often prescribed medications simply to keep up with the fast-paced schedule. Despite this, children seemed to grow sicker, and parents' needs became increasingly complex. Conditions like Autism, ADHD, anxiety, and depression were on the rise, as were diseases like asthma, eczema, and obesity. I grew frustrated and disheartened as patient needs escalated while the time available for their care did not. At the same time, the administrative workload and paperwork requirements increased to satisfy insurance carriers and corporate demands.

Occasionally, in the office, I couldn't help but cringe when overhearing comments from the staff or witnessing the overtly judgmental, divisive, and sometimes racist treatment of families. Looking back, I wish I had expressed more contempt for such unacceptable behavior. Regrettably, it seemed woven into our office's toxic and accepted culture. Acceptance was reserved for families who shared similar ideals and cultures. At the same time, under-the-breath comments abounded for those with different cultural expectations of healthcare, those who questioned recommendations, those who sought alternative options, or those who made different choices in raising their children or regarding certain medications or vaccinations. This culture of conformity affected how patients were treated and how we treated each other to the point where I sometimes dreaded going to work.

This would all spill into my personal life. After feeling completely depleted after my workday, I would then go home to three children who also needed me. After listening to patient complaints all day, if my children had complaints or needs when I got home, I often simply would not have the capacity to give in the way I would have liked to. It was like every caring bone in my body was sucked out of me. And my own needs were unmet, as well. Then, I would feel frustrated, guilty, and ashamed for not being the parent I should be. There are some discussions about burnout and compassion fatigue for healthcare providers, but I have heard very little about how it extends into their personal lives and relationships with their loved ones. As time went on, and mainly in the later part of my career, when I had my own practice, I gained more tools to handle this better. But I still grieve the seemingly lost time with my children when they were young. I feel it would be helpful and supportive for care providers to bring more light and attention to this area.

Journal Prompt

In what ways have you felt frustrated in your personal or professional life and know something needs to change? Have you ever felt trapped in a situation but know there is a better way? You might have several things to say or just one defining moment. It can be minor or significant, or anything in between. It doesn't matter; whatever comes up is perfect.

CHAPTER 3

A Healing Awakening: My Path to Integrative Medicine

"I found the greatest love of all inside of me."

—Lyrics from the song "The Greatest Love of All" by Linda Creed (1977)

I am very grateful and respectful of what modern Western medicine offers us. I will never forget baby Nala.[1] Nala fell off the changing table at daycare, so mom was called and notified, but she otherwise seemed to be acting okay. Her mother called our office and spoke with the nurse. The nurse advised mom to watch her but not to worry, as this was not an uncommon phone call to receive in pediatrics.

A few hours later, in the late afternoon, mom called back. She was more worried now. She said Nala was sleepier than usual and wanted her to be seen at the office. She was squeezed into my schedule at the end of a hectic, jam-packed day. I happened to be standing near the front desk when they walked in, and I saw the look on mom's face. She was panicked and said that Nala was not responding to her. We ushered her quickly to an exam room and took the child out of the car seat and onto the exam table. She was unarousable, pale, and lifeless. My heart dropped. I will never forget that moment. I'm sure the mother never will either.

---

1 The name, Nala, has been changed for privacy.

We immediately called the ambulance and the children's hospital to inform them about the child. I remember holding the mother as she was sobbing while we waited for the arrival of the EMTs. It felt like hours, even though it was minutes. When they arrived at the emergency room, the neurosurgeon was there to evaluate her and immediately brought her into surgery, as she had a life-threatening intracranial bleed.

Later that evening, I received a call saying that she had come out of surgery successfully, but if there had been any more of a delay before her emergency surgery, she might not have made it. It was a miracle. I cried tears of joy and relief.

I followed Nala and her family for several more years before I left the practice, and she grew into a beautiful, completely developmentally normal, wonderful little girl.

Without the advancements of Western medicine, emergency preparedness, swift response, and the brilliance of our doctors and our emergency medical system, this might not have been the outcome. I am truly grateful.

A Different Approach

Alongside my immense gratitude and appreciation for conventional Western medicine, my interest in holistic medicine and energy healing grew throughout my career. I have always been fascinated with energy healing, especially its elusiveness and mystery. The world of energy healing is difficult to analyze and discuss because it is so cosmic and spiritual in nature. There is plenty of science, research, and literature in vast support of it, but for me, it is not as important because it is experiential.

My first exposure to energy healing was in the 90s, during my undergraduate nursing preparation. The most memorable part of my four years of nursing school was the mere two hours we spent learning about Therapeutic Touch, developed by Delores Krieger, PhD, RN, in the 1970s.

After becoming a nurse practitioner, I enrolled in a Reiki healing training course to deepen my knowledge of holistic medicine. The experience was powerful and one of my first and most significant steps toward the love and dedication to alternative healing practices. I use Reiki regularly on myself and sometimes on my children and patients, and I know the deep rewards on a subtle, energetic level. I remain in awe of how the human body can have so many complex, intricate structures all working together within one system of balance and regulation.

My later training in Cranial Sacral Therapy (CST) through Upledger Institute led me to an even deeper understanding of how the intricacies of the body are all connected and are all energy. Everything affects everything else. This is universally true as well. My favorite Native American proverb from Chief Seattle in 1854 hangs in my bedroom as it resonates so profoundly:

"Humankind has not woven the web of life. We are but one thread within it. Whatever we do to the web, we do to ourselves. All things are bound together. All things connect."

Indigenous Native American cultures have a deeply spiritual understanding of health and healing that weaves in purification rituals and ceremony for healing of the mind, body and soul. Ayurvedic medicine is an ancient healing system from India that uses natural and holistic approaches to prevent and treat illness by maintaining balance in the body, mind and consciousness. Chinese medicine also has a beautiful understanding of how emotional, physical, and spiritual dynamics organize us within ourselves, with each other, and in nature. In harmony, we have health; in disharmony, we have disease and suffering. The healing practice of acupuncture is rooted in ancient Chinese medicine and culture, and the treatment facilitates the body's healing from imbalances and addresses obstruction of life force, or *qi*. For a deeper dive into ancient Chinese medicine, I highly recommend *Between Heaven and Earth* by Harriet Beinfield and Efrem Korngold. In contrast to Western medicine, which looks at the body and disease in parts, organs, and symptoms that are identified and treated separately, Acupuncture and Chinese medicine are designed to support *qi* to flow freely in the body, therefore reducing physical disease and disharmony.

The Intersection of Spirituality and Religion

I grew up Quaker, thanks to my hippie parents (I'm paying homage). They went to college in the 1960s, found each other during this historical time of rebellion and the Vietnam War, veered away from their conservative Christian doctrine-filled upbringing, and found Quakerism together. As

I reflect on integrative medicine, I am struck by some parallels with the philosophy and birth of Quakerism. The religion was founded in the 17th century by George Fox during religious turmoil in England when people sought reform. Quakerism is a Christian religion, but this is commonly not understood. The name officially became the Religious Society of Friends. Fox felt that the presence of God was found within people, every person, rather than only inside churches and church leaders. Even though many others shared his views, and the movement was growing, Fox was seen by some as a threat to society and was jailed for blasphemy in 1650. Quakers' views were considered radical, such as the idea that men and women were spiritual equals. Quakers didn't have official ministers or religious rituals. Later, in the 1600s, they were forced to flee England to escape religious persecution, mainly because the leaders publicly challenged the English class system.

Quakers have a firm belief in equality and commitment to community. They believe that we all are equal in the eyes of God. They were pivotal in the women's suffrage movement and the fight to abolish slavery. The dedication has continued, and many "modern-day" Quakers still champion social justice and human rights. In Quaker services, there is no Minister. No one person is the expert; no one person is superior to anyone else. You are not told what to think or do during their religious services. You sit in "silent worship." You are your own connection to the spirit. They believe in an individual's "inner light" or conscience to guide their spiritual connection. You can speak if you feel moved to during worship. You can pray. You can meditate. You can pray to God. You can pray to Goddess. You can pray to Buddha. You can pray to Allah. You can pray to the Universe. The religion attracts all kinds of people because of their righteous belief in acceptance. Famous Quakers include Herbert Hoover, Richard Nixon, James Michener, Judi Dench, James Dean, Bonnie Raitt, and Joan Baez. A Quaker way of life emphasizes simplicity, integrity, and equality.

More recently, I have been studying and deepening with the gnostic gospels and the Cathar teachings. The Cathars were a Christian community in Southern France in the 12th century who rejected the teachings of the Roman Catholic Church. Instead, they regarded the teachings of Jesus Christ (Yeshua) and Mary Magdalene. Much of Mary Magdalene's story was erased, and the bits we have been told were maligned and downright lied about. For years, western Christianity depicted Mary Magdalene as a former prostitute. This narrative began in the 6th century with Pope Gregory the Great. Because of undeniable evidence and increasing awareness, including the "sudden" discovery in 1945 of ancient texts in the Egyptian town of Nag Hammadi, in 1960, the Catholic church had to admit their wrongdoings about her story and redeemed Mary Magdalene in the truth of who she really was, and later naming her the "Apostle of the Apostles" as well as declaring July 22 as her Feast Day.

The Cathars lived less with the ego and more in the "Way of Love." They were believed to have lived simply, had no possessions, imposed no tax or penalties, and regarded men and women as equals. They risked their lives to recognize each other as equals, innately worthy of love, no matter their status. Between the years 1209 and 1213, an estimated half million men, women, and children were all victims of a horrendous and tragic genocidal massacre led by the Inquisition of the Roman Catholic Church for "heresy" and a refusal to acknowledge the pope as their leader. With the massacre of the people came the burning and destruction of their artifacts and documents, leading to our unfortunate lack of information about them. And, of course, horrifically, many other groups of people, religions, and cultures have faced rejection and persecution in our history and still do to this day.

The integration of conventional Western medicine and holistic medicine (integrative medicine) is not a rejection of science and medical advances but rather a deepened investigation into health that medical science may not fully explain. Integrative medicine also recognizes what science already fully understands but may overlook or not be valued in our current, fast-paced healthcare crisis. Human needs are not a "one size fits all" category. And there is not just one right way to do things. And not just one leader can dictate how to do things. Since every person's biochemistry is uniquely different, what works for one person will not always work for the next. This can sometimes clash with a Western doctor's training to give this medicine for that disease or to administer this test to diagnose that problem. The concept that the body can heal itself is vital and real. This can threaten some traditional patriarchal medical training that emphasizes the cavalier heroic doctor who is needed to treat the sick. Health and healing should be an interaction or interplay between the client and the healer.

While the Quakers and Cathars didn't reject Christianity and their faith in the divine, they did reject the constraints of their religious expression and pressure to bow to the Church of England and the Roman Catholic Church, respectively. They faced the fear of persecution, torture, and imprisonment and often had to leave their homes and countries, but they remained steadfast in their beliefs and morals, flourished, and created new ways of thinking and living.

Pursuing Holistic Education

A few years into my career, I enrolled in a graduate-level Integrative Health and Healing program. I was incorporating holistic health into the care of my patients as much as I could, but I wanted to learn how to enhance it even further. During this time, not only did I learn about many different modalities of health and healing, but I also really took the time to do the work of reflection and understanding myself. Through our coursework and writings, we were challenged to dig deeply into patterns of dysfunction in order to grow and become who we really wanted to be in this world. This was a significant time for me. And I am very grateful for the opportunity and how it has influenced me as a provider.

Facing a Career Crossroads

A few years before I left my job at the pediatric office, I vividly remember getting a text from my friend in the middle of the workday. She enthusiastically informed me that the legislation had finally passed in Connecticut, allowing an APRN to practice independently after three years of collaborative practice with an MD. At the time, I thought it was really awesome, but how could I possibly do something like going out on my own? I could never do that! My skills and expertise were in clinical and patient care. I knew very little about running a business or the administrative side of healthcare. And I needed the security of the job and benefits. I thought I couldn't provide holistic, integrative care while financially supporting myself and my children. I thought I needed the structure of the patriarchal healthcare paradigm in order to practice as a pediatric APRN. We were taught nothing about business or leadership in nursing school—neither undergraduate nor graduate. Are you seeing a pattern of self-doubt and self-sabotage here? In retrospect, I feel this is ingrained and intentional since nurses and advanced practice nurses are still taught within a patriarchal construct. We are supposed to work for doctors and larger healthcare corporations. It was incorporated into our training. There were no teachings about running your practice or business, being a leader in your field, or practicing independently. I didn't even consider this until I was conversing with my current business partner, a naturopathic doctor. When she was in ND school, they actually did receive some classes and instructions on these essential principles.

I still was feeling stuck and frustrated. Yet, over the course of another few years, I increasingly longed for something else. I was becoming more curious and more bold; something was stewing in me. I knew there was something else for me. I knew deep down that I had a higher calling and purpose to provide care, which I knew in my heart was better for children and families and, ultimately, better for me. I was thriving and achieving in my current office, but I felt like a factory worker and was dissatisfied. Emerging from a "dark night of the soul," I was ready to be reborn into a more authentic version of myself. I needed to reclaim myself.

A Shift Toward Authenticity and Independence

I came across an ad in a local holistic magazine looking for different types of healthcare providers. A Naturopathic Doctor was expanding her solo practice and starting an Integrative Medicine office with the hopes of several different types of practitioners working together collaboratively. We all would be working as independent contractors under one roof. She would provide the business side of things, which was a relief because, at the time, I felt that I knew nothing about business or being a business owner. It felt like a great opportunity, a dream come true, the one I had longed for all this time! So, I followed my desires, quit my "stable" job—even though I was scared as hell—and started to figure out how to set up my practice and grow my business.

Much to my delight and surprise, my patient base grew quickly. I was figuring out how to handle the administrative side of things while, most importantly, providing quality care. It was an invaluable experience, but not without its unforeseen pitfalls. My expectations of what it would be did not quite come to fruition. I did not feel valued or respected, even though

I brought a lot of business into the office. I saw things from a very different perspective and had significant differences in opinion from the owner of the practice. Within the first year or two, I realized this would not work for me long term, even though I loved my patients and felt very committed to them. I had already put in a lot of time, energy, and monetary investment. I was crushed.

I then spoke with a friend and colleague who also had an integrative medicine practice about possibly joining her. We ultimately realized that it wouldn't work out for several reasons. But I remember very clearly when she said, "You should open your own practice, Lara. You could totally do it!" After some more fretting, praying, and dissolving of my ego, I ultimately decided that was exactly what I needed to do. Just do it, Lara, GEEZ!

The Value of Trusted Pediatric Providers

I have come across some "holistic mom" social media groups and have seen a disturbing trend of recommendations to never bring your child to the doctor, even for wellness exams. These women have had such bad experiences that they chose just to stay away from the healthcare industry entirely, as well as recommend that others do the same unless it is a true emergency. I find this to be very sad and often not ultimately in the child's and family's best interests. It is heartbreaking that our healthcare system has created this kind of distrust. Honestly, I can understand why some people feel this way, after some of the stories I have heard. I appreciate and respect that moms can find like-minded communities to ask questions and support each other in these groups. Parenting is tough, and it is essential to feel supported and connected in any way you can. However, I also firmly believe that having a trusted pediatrician from birth is important and hugely beneficial.

When you regularly bring your child in for wellness exams, a professional relationship is developed, and the child's healthcare provider gets to know the history of your child's history, your family's history, and how you operate as a family unit. Specific issues can be addressed earlier so they don't become bigger issues later. When more acute or urgent situations arise, your healthcare provider will then be able to more quickly and thoroughly access and treat you in an individualized manner. When children don't feel well, their behaviors are often understandably worse and unpredictable. The physical exam of a sick child is usually very helpful in determining a quick diagnosis, but if a stranger in a strange place is examining your child when they don't feel well, it often leads to crying and resistance, and sometimes even screaming and hitting. If you are seeing an already established and familiar provider, the exam may go smoother. Not always, but it might help! Pediatric providers are very used to and often very skilled at evaluating difficult and crying patients, but exams can go much better for everyone if this is not the case. A relationship with a trusted provider also sets the stage for children to know what to look for and expect as they become adults navigating their own healthcare.

Crafting a Vision for Pediatric Care

After I decided to completely "set up shop" on my own, I was talking to a dear friend who was also a pediatric provider. She asked me, "What do you want your office to be like? Why are you really doing this?" I started to rattle off all the things I didn't want for my practice, and the list was getting pretty long. She stopped me and said, "No, don't tell me what you don't want; envision what you DO want!" That made me pause and reframe. It became clear to me that what I really wanted was a pediatric office that families *want* to come to! Where they actually look forward to sharing their health journeys with me and where the kids feel safe, loved, and nurtured. A place where all families of race, religion, culture, values, and choices can come and feel accepted, valued, and free to ask questions and have open discussions. I know what it is like to feel misunderstood and unseen. I never want children to have to go through that or feel that way, at least on my watch. I wanted an office where I could really make a difference in the health and vitality of these children and their families. It felt liberating and exciting to have this clarity.

Journal Prompt

Were there experiences or moments in the earlier part of your career or parenting that you feel shaped you significantly or elicited change? Have you ever felt frustrated or disempowered and felt that you couldn't express yourself in the way you wish you could? You might have several things to say here or just one defining moment. It could be minor or significant, or everything in between. It doesn't matter; whatever comes up is perfect.

CHAPTER 4

Integrating Holistic Medicine: Gone Rogue

"I decided long ago never to walk in anyone's shadow. If I fail, if I succeed, at least I'll live as I believe."

—Lyrics from the song "The Greatest Love of All" by Linda Creed (1977)

I opened my own practice in 2018 and started the endeavor of building what I always wanted: to give the pediatric care that I truly believed families and children needed. I was blessed with finding another Naturopathic Doctor who shared my visions and wanted to grow her own integrative family practice the way I did. The services we provided also complemented each other. The partnership naturally evolved into an integrative family wellness center. We incorporated other complementary services and providers in the office, as well. It was very exhilarating, and it was also very challenging, but we were up for it!

We Go Up, and We Go Down... and Up Again

Often in life, when things are going swimmingly, you get tested. Yeah, that's right, a wedge in the plans, something to shake you up a little. It almost feels like the universe likes to throw something at you just to make damn sure that you really got this, that you are not just dipping a toe in. I have learned—albeit the hard way—that whenever you make a big pivot in your life to follow your heart and soul's purpose, it is never easy. Disrupting the status quo—lovingly called the "Big Snooze" in Jen Sincero's *You're a Badass*—is usually followed by chaos. The ego vehemently does not like change. It is a journey of fortitude, perseverance, and faith. I experienced this after my divorce when I had three young children. First, the sewage drain clogged and my basement literally filled up with shit. How is that for a metaphor!? A few months later, when I went downstairs to make breakfast for the girls before getting them to school and rushing to work, I discovered that the ceiling had fallen on top of my kitchen table. Yes, the CEILING on top of my KITCHEN TABLE. I was paralyzed with overwhelm. It felt like the world had fallen on top of my head. I wanted to curl up in a ball and cry for hours. But the girls were staring at me. They needed to get to school. I needed to get to work. I needed to get the ceiling off of my table. So, there was no room for wallowing in my misery. Yup, I hear you chuckling, that might be a bit dramatic, but I know you know what I am talking about.

Fast forward several years later after I opened my practice. I got sick—it was pretty bad. It started with rotating aches and pains throughout my body for several months, but I had chalked it up to stress and getting older. First, my shoulder, then my hand, and then my foot, all on the right side. Do you know how "older people" love to tell you about how things start to hurt when you get older? Well, I thought it was that. Or at least, I was willing to believe it was so I could keep on going and basically ignore it. And I felt that I didn't have time to slow down and pay attention (hint: never the best idea).

I guess this is confession time. I am a really bad patient. I rarely go to the doctor, and if I do, I often don't take their advice or recommendations, or at least completely. Okay, I said it. Yes, I see the irony.

But then it got worse. I started feeling really exhausted—more than usual. I was used to being tired: single mother of three, business owner with a full practice of hundreds of patients, *blah, blah, blah.* But this was unusually tired for me, even worse than when I had newborn twins and a three-year-old! And that was bad, trust me. This was a different kind of tired; this was an extreme down-to-the bone fatigue that went deeper than just not getting enough sleep.

Then, one busy day at work, I went to the bathroom, washed my hands, and BAM, I got horribly dizzy with a headache. I had to brace myself on the counter to regain balance. I stumbled downstairs to where there was a massage room to lay down for a few minutes to try to regain composure before my next patient arrived. Unfortunately, it never got much better, and I suffered for another few months in hopes that it would resolve. But the dizziness, headaches, inability to focus, and brain fog only intensified.

One day, I was with a three-year-old boy and his mother, and the child was making very loud noises with a plastic toy by repeatedly throwing it off the exam table and letting it crash onto the floor. This was something that I was used to in all my years working with children, as well as with my own! But this time, the noise was like an electric current shooting through my body. It created a debilitating headache, like a "closing in" of my brain. At that moment, I succumbed. I couldn't keep this up. I realized I needed to seek care.

Turned out it was Lyme disease. After my diagnosis, the memory of about four months prior came hauntingly back to me... It was a gorgeous sunny day in the fall, and we had gone on a hike in Vermont. At the top of the mountain, I laid down in the grass and practically fell asleep. It seemed like a wonderful idea at the time... But maybe not so much.

Being the "bad patient" that I am, I had ignored the early symptoms. Once I was diagnosed, all my alarm bells started ringing because I had treated Lyme for many years in my patients, and I knew how bad it could be. The longer it went on undiagnosed and untreated, the worse the disease usually was. I felt shame about getting sick since I was the one who was supposed to be helping sick people! I felt shame about delaying my diagnosis by ignoring the symptoms. And since I was not feeling well, I knew that I couldn't be the best care provider that I strive to be. I had to take care of myself and get better—as fast as possible.

So, my healing journey began, but those many months were very challenging. I realized just how much I gave to my patients and how important it was for me to be healthy and feel good myself in order to do so. I dedicated myself to embodying my knowledge of how the body heals with rest, stress reduction, energy medicine, prayer, surrender, nutrition, plant medicine, homeopathy, and targeted supplementation. I was blessed with the support of friends, colleagues, and healers, who were well-versed in how to treat Lyme. I am fortunate enough to say that I was able to recover, but it took many months. And even for a few years after my recovery, if I was under a lot of physical or even emotional stress, some of the symptoms would return, as if to remind me to slow down and nurture myself.

It was a humbling experience because my life didn't stop just because I was feeling absolutely lousy. I was still a single mother of three. I was still a business owner. And I still had a lot of patients who relied on me for their care. These roles were very important to me. They defined me. I cherish them. I am an independent, can-do-it-all-on-my-own kind of gal, but to be honest, there were many tears behind closed doors—a lot of frustration, doubt, and victimhood. I gave every bit of energy and brain capacity that I had when I was in the office. Time with my family suffered. Time for myself suffered. There were days of despair and utter exhaustion. But I also learned a lot about myself. It was my chance for deep inner exploration and wake-up calls. I worked on some things that I needed to let go of. It is easy to be present for patients when I am feeling well because that is what I love to do. But when I was sick and bone-tired, it was very challenging and brought up my demons, so to speak.

I struggled deeply with feeling vulnerable, with not-good-enoughness, and with feelings of failure. It dismantled my life and how I functioned on a daily basis. I needed to allow myself to be sick without the feeling of shame, and I needed to allow my body to heal. This was hard for me because it is not my natural tendency, but I had no choice. Just as I would speak with my patients about ways to rest and nurture themselves, I needed to heed my own advice. So, I created a lighter schedule. Sometimes, I needed to nap in the afternoon. I often fell asleep on the couch as soon as I got home. I sought out help from several types of healers. I relied on my family and loved ones to help more. I created better boundaries. All along, I knew this was an opportunity for reflection and growth and that this experience would shape me to serve others. Shamanic healing teaches us to go into curiosity and ask ourselves, "Why did I script this?" In my case, it was to teach me the importance of listening to my body's inner wisdom. To help me be a better healer and to have more empathy for myself and others. I gained an even deeper understanding of people with chronic disease and chronic stress.

Reframing Past Struggles

Years earlier, when I was staffed in the pediatric office, I went through a divorce. It was emotionally devastating and exhausting, but I never showed it at work or took any time off for myself, except for the one day that I had to go to court. I "held it all together" because I felt that was important to do for my career and for my patients, as well as my children. I didn't allow myself to fully feel what I was experiencing because it was too hard, and I was worried that I would completely fall apart if I did so. A few months later, my boss actually commended me for not allowing my divorce to create any repercussions in my work. I was surprised that he was even aware or cared. And at that moment, I felt proud and acknowledged. But reflecting back, I realized that it really hurt me inside to carry on like everything was normal. It actually did adversely affect my children and my job. I had many repressed emotions and deep pain. I was exhausted. It just didn't outwardly show because I didn't slow down or take any time off, and that was the only thing that was rewarded and valued.

Physical, spiritual, and emotional stress all affect our ultimate health. How I emotionally handled my divorce in the beginning led to greater suffering. But how I handled having Lyme disease ultimately led me to greater healing. I also became a better care provider and have a new level of understanding of chronic disease and feelings of helplessness and vulnerability. Health is not just the absence of disease. It is much more multifactorial and nuanced.

The Art of Medicine

How Doctors Think is a unique book by Jerome Groopman, M.D. Dr. Groopman explores and sheds light on healthcare and medical thinking as a delicate balance of science and art. He uses research, interviews with some of the country's best doctors, and intriguing real-life situations to explore how doctors think, the relationship between provider and client, some dangerous pitfalls, and recommendations that are beneficial to both the healthcare provider and the healthcare seeker.

Better by Atul Gawande, MD is also an interesting and gripping book written by a practicing surgeon about the subtle intricacies and the larger complexities of medicine. The challenge of medicine is to always do better, improve, and learn. Mistakes and room for growth are a part of every field, but in medicine, the double-edged sword of error can directly affect a human life. Dr. Gawande compassionately examines several areas of medicine, including the less talked about and taboo subjects such as examining someone naked, hand washing, and financial, political, and emotional influences on medicine. My favorite quote in the book is, "And that in itself is evidence of how much we've underestimated the importance and difficulty of human interactions in medicine."

In traditional medical training and practice, there is no support for individual understanding or self-inquiry into inner feelings and emotional states. Doctors are trained to think intellectually, evidence-based, and systematically, but the problem is that it is not possible for a human being to operate without emotional attachment or judgment. Doctors are not trained or encouraged to acknowledge this, let alone explore how it affects them. One needs to be robotic and scripted to function in this realm. But humans are not scripted; they do not line up to follow textbook explanations. And I believe it leads to the disconnect that patients often feel with their providers.

The truth is that we are all just humans taking care of humans despite our training, education, and experience. We all make mistakes, and we all have shortcomings. It's important that we are able to critically and honestly look at our judgments, prejudices, and past traumas so that we don't "bring it to the table," so to speak, and we allow the opportunity to grow and learn from these experiences.

I've always felt it was important to read about and understand many different cultures, traditions, religions, and ways of thinking that are different from my own. My mother did a wonderful job of exposing me to many religions while I was growing up, as well as teaching and embodying love and acceptance.

The "art of science and medicine" is nuanced, and we are not typically taught about it or encouraged to think about it in our training and education. It would be like asking an engineer about the "art of engineering." It is just not in our framework, but regardless, it is a very important aspect to consider. Especially in this day and age of artificial intelligence medicine, this is something that is in stark contrast. We are gaining scientific knowledge and technological advancements at warp speed, which is amazing. There are huge benefits to this, as well as massive potential shortcomings. Artificial intelligence in medicine may have some advantages, but we also need human interaction with a provider who has wisdom, creativity, compassion, empathy, and intuition. There is a time and place, just like everything. I may be just one small voice, but I know many others feel the same; let's keep the ART and HEART in medicine and healing.

Disrupting the Medical Matrix

While I was working in the traditional Pediatric office, my boss explained that he usually makes his diagnosis, or at least whether or not to be concerned, in the first five seconds of a patient encounter. He is a brilliant and very experienced doctor, which is true and valuable in today's practice of medicine. Honestly, he was usually completely right. But this also has potentially dangerous pitfalls. Patients can become their own advocates by understanding this and how to navigate through it.

In primary care, we see many patients daily, sometimes with monotony. The concern is that as it becomes routine, you can stop observing closely. There have been evenings after a busy day when a patient will pop into my head. I may worry about something overlooked or an incorrect diagnosis. I make sure to always say to families, "Does this make sense to you?" or "Please don't hesitate to call back if your child gets worse, displays X, Y, or Z, or just doesn't get better." Sometimes, I even call to check in the next day or two.

Since the beginning of my career, I have tried very hard to do a good and thorough job, with compassion and kindness towards families, coupled with sound medical decision-making. I eagerly awaited any advice on how to improve. But the only feedback I got in the traditional allopathic setting was the importance of going faster and seeing more patients in a day. Within our current health insurance framework, the unfortunate thing is that the only way for primary care practitioners to sustain a prosperous and sustainable office is from volume. Because of insurance companies' dictation and complicated billing systems, reimbursement is often very low, and the burnout from taking care of patient after patient is very high.

This is partially why I became disenchanted with traditional Western medical practices. However, I do believe that integrative medicine is "breathing some life" back into our current healthcare crisis, as well as greatly benefiting both doctors' and patients' ability to collaborate towards better outcomes. But this will continue to take change, awareness, and consciousness on many levels. Along the way, we seem to have collectively lost trust in our own body's immune system and wisdom. Integrative medicine gives us more tools so that we can actually do something to help. We need to give our patients hope and trust in their resilience, and in doing so, we alleviate fear.

New York Times opinion columnist Ross Douthat joins in the conversation about the problems with our healthcare system, especially when it comes to chronic illness, in his provocative memoir about his struggles with chronic Lyme disease in *The Hidden Places.* He calls upon physicians to be more willing to approach medical treatments as "not just a science but a difficult, interesting, experimental art."

I love Dr. Patch Adams' description: "The art of medicine comes from the intuition and inherent magic found in compassion, love, humor, wonder and curiosity." The art of medicine has as much value as the science of medicine but is far too often overlooked and devalued in Western education and practice. Exploring other cultural and ancestral frameworks for definitions of health, healing, and disease has offered me a deeper understanding of this.

I am grateful for the stark differences between my mother and father and my life experiences, as they helped me understand and balance the feminine/masculine duality principles of mystery, intuition, compassion, and magic with productivity, achievement, and practicality. Thereby contributing to the skill of using both the art and science of medicine and healing.

Pediatric Healthcare

Pediatric healthcare comes with its own set of challenges. Your patient isn't just the child, but is also the parent or caregiver, which can lead to complexities and nuances. Sometimes, kids have weird symptoms like a rash or a cough, yet otherwise look good. A good provider must be comfortable monitoring and educating about supportive care and the signs and symptoms to watch for, which would warrant more action or concern. Education and experience of the provider are valuable, but "knowing" or intuition is also an integral part of the healing process and is certainly not often discussed in traditional medical training. Maternal instinct and intuition should always be acknowledged, listened to, and revered. Integrative medicine provides more "tools in our belt" to help support children and parents through some of these circumstances. In all my years of practice, I will have to say that sometimes kids just "do the darndest things" that we otherwise don't have the best explanation for, especially a medical explanation, but otherwise don't have any potential for long-term harm and usually "resolve" on their own. Feeling comfortable with this prevents over-medicalization and intervention. Unfortunately, over-medicalization is often based on a fear of liability and an area in healthcare that needs attention. However, a skilled clinician must also know when symptoms or presentations warrant more immediate action and modern medicine intervention. Pediatrics is really interesting in this way, and not for the faint-hearted.

Our Children's Health Crisis

It is glaringly obvious that we have a crisis in our children's health. Statistics on chronic disease for children are staggering. In my thirty years of practice, I have noticed a significant difference. There are increasing numbers of children with issues like asthma, allergies, obesity, inflammatory bowel disease, autoimmune disease, and mental health issues. Our world is full of toxins, often unregulated, in our food, medications, and environment. It shouldn't be this way. Why are we accepting this? Many other countries have stricter regulations regarding these issues than the United States. We are seeing many more autistic children than ever before. In 2023, the CDC reported that approximately 1 in 36 children in the U.S. is diagnosed with an autism spectrum disorder (ASD), according to 2020 data. What will happen to these children when they are young adults? Older adults? And what about support for their caregivers? We must be willing to ask ourselves "why?" but that isn't happening enough. And I don't believe for one second that it is just because we are diagnosing them better now.

The Best of Both Worlds

In my humble opinion, integrative medicine has the best "both worlds" approach. I am grateful for my training in modern medicine and what it offers. In emergencies, our hospitals and ERs are equipped with brilliant doctors and nurses, lifesaving technology, and complex and innovative care. I am so appreciative and reverent for this. In the primary care setting, I can help a child in acute circumstances like an asthma attack with albuterol and steroids, treat an infection with antibiotics when necessary, order bloodwork or imaging to help aid in the diagnosis and create a treatment plan. But more often than not, I rely on natural treatments to address minor health issues, provide lifestyle education and support, offer guidance on complementary care, and take a holistic approach to uncover the root causes of diseases. I steer clear of excessive use of prescription medications for symptom relief. Instead, I aim to bring about tangible positive changes that significantly impact long-term health and overall well-being. After all, it is not important whether you fall but whether you get up again.

Integrative Health Solutions

Case 1: Parasitic Infections and Natural Remedies

A personal example of using integrative medicine is when my daughter developed intermittent, chronic stomach pains, nausea, and diarrhea after returning home from a school trip to Costa Rica. After some failed attempts to treat her symptoms, I became increasingly suspicious of a parasite. We did functional medicine stool testing, which confirmed it. Since the symptoms had been going on for a while, she was pretty sick at this point and had significant weight loss, I attempted to treat it with the recommended prescription medication. Unfortunately, this made her so violently ill that we ended up in the emergency room, needing IV fluids and anti-nausea medication to stop the intractable vomiting. So, we ditched the pharmaceutical and continued with targeted natural treatments, herbs, homeopathy, nutraceuticals, and diet in collaboration with our naturopathic physician, and it resolved after a couple of months.

Case 2: Knee Pain and Alternative Treatments

My middle child struggled with chronic intermittent knee pain for several years. After initially ruling out Lyme disease and other inflammatory causes, seeing an orthopedic doctor, and getting an X-ray, we started working with a pediatric chiropractor. She was diagnosed with patellofemoral syndrome and was taught exercises to do at home to strengthen her weaker quadriceps, as well as six weeks of physical therapy. When she has discomfort, she uses homeopathy and essential oils to help alleviate the pain. Throughout the years and as she continued to grow, the pain returned a few times, especially with sports, so we saw our chiropractor, who evaluated her and applied Neurokinetic Therapy (NKT), which has helped to alleviate the issue. More recently, she has also used massage and acupuncture, which helps significantly.

Case 3: Scoliosis and Chiropractic Care

My oldest daughter was diagnosed with scoliosis when she was about 13. I knew that for mild to moderate scoliosis, there wasn't much offered beyond monitoring as the child grew, potentially consulting with Orthopedics and possibly bracing, which had limited effectiveness. If her scoliosis had been more severe, I would have opted for the more traditional route. Instead, I brought her to a Chiropractor trained in treating scoliosis in children. The scoliosis improved through chiropractic treatments, targeted exercises at home, and Pilates. This was a much better outcome than her having to endure the physical discomfort, along with the self-consciousness of bracing, especially at her age. Of course, it was much preferable to surgery.

Alternative Approaches to Common Health Issues

Case 4: Recurrent Ear Infections

I had a family who transferred to me when their youngest son was a toddler. He already had a history of multiple ear infections and many courses of antibiotics, and his doctors were talking about having myringotomy surgery to have ear tubes placed to help prevent future ear infections from developing. The family was motivated to help him, hopefully avoiding surgery and reducing his ear infections. We discussed his health history, diet, nutrition, and what the parents had already tried to help him. We changed his diet, took out dairy, added chiropractic support, and started using natural treatments at the start of colds, congestion, or suspicion of ear infections. Several years later, I am happy to report that he is doing great and has not had any more ear infections requiring antibiotics. He did not require surgery. This story is not uncommon. Sometimes, antibiotics are needed for serious ear infections. Sometimes, surgery for ear tubes is the best choice in those circumstances. But it is not the only option, even though it is often the only treatment discussed in traditional pediatric offices.

Case 5: PANDAS Diagnosis

I had a family who started seeing me when one of their daughters was ten years old. She had a significant mental health history and had two psychiatric inpatient hospital stays that past year. The family had a history of stress and trauma, so initially, it was thought to be attributed to this. The mother reported that she was "very volatile; fine one minute, then violent the next." She was clingy and fearful and expressed homicidal and suicidal ideation. She was often happy and energetic, but when she had a flare, she would become sluggish, depressed, and irritable.

Mom researched and started learning about PANDAS (Pediatric Autoimmune Neuropsychiatric Disorder Associated with Streptococcal Infections). When she asked her pediatrician about it, she was told, "It's not a real thing." So, the mother decided to seek help elsewhere and found me. Her daughter was currently in outpatient therapy and on an antidepressant medication. She was diagnosed with Autism at age six, but with a recent neuropsychiatric evaluation, the diagnosis was removed and was changed to a mood disorder, ADHD, and PTSD, with a question of anxiety and OCD as well.

Three things really caught my attention about her story. One was that the mother noticed her daughter's behaviors improved when taking ibuprofen. She also reported that she had discovered that her daughter had urinated on a pile of clothes in her bedroom. The third was that she noticed improved mood, behaviors, and energy when she was on antibiotics. We did extensive blood work and found contributing factors, including increased antibody titers in a few infectious sources such as strep. The treatment plan involved an extended course of antibiotics and some dietary changes, natural supplementation, and neurofeedback. Six weeks later, she had remarkable improvements in her mood, behaviors, and energy. A year later, she had another event with suicidal ideation and self-harm and was hospitalized again. After an evaluation, it was discovered that several family members had a strep infection, and she had elevated titers again. She was back on her treatment plan and improved again. To this day, it is absolutely baffling that there are doctors who are still dismissive of patients who inquire about a possible diagnosis of PANS/ PANDAS. It is far more common than we realize, and there is plenty of research and a solid understanding of the pathophysiology, as well as educational opportunities for clinicians. I truly believe that numerous pediatric patients who are diagnosed with a mental health disease could benefit greatly from an evaluation to look at possible infectious sources contributing to their brain inflammation.

Case 6: Dietary Changes

Many of my patients who had previously struggled with symptoms like rashes, stomach pains, headaches, and even behavioral issues have resolved or significantly improved these conditions with dietary changes or by eliminating certain trigger foods. Gluten and dairy are very high on that list. It never ceases to amaze me how these simple changes are often overlooked and sometimes even overtly dismissed by traditional doctors. Countless Americans are on prescription medications, which carry significant side effects and could have otherwise been treated with a dietary change. I find that to be alarming and downright sad. The quality of our food has a lot to do with this, as well as our over-reliance on processed foods, lack of regulation on the food industry for the sake of profit, and doctors' general lack of nutrition education. It's actually embarrassing.

Case 7: Underlying Causes of Eczema

I have encountered a huge number of kids in my practice who struggle with eczema (atopic dermatitis). In fact, it seems to be on the rise like never before. Earlier in my career, you would see it every once in a while. Now, it seems to have become more the norm, sadly to say. I have also noticed that it has become more difficult to treat. It is commonly addressed by pediatricians and dermatologists with steroid creams, which offer temporary relief but do not address the root cause of the problem. Moreover, there are long-term detrimental effects of using steroid cream on the skin. I certainly resort to using steroid creams in the short term if absolutely necessary, and the child is suffering while I attempt to determine the underlying cause. Eczema is not uncommonly triggered by a food sensitivity, an allergy, an irritant, or even gut dysbiosis. These triggers can be successfully treated by identifying them, making the necessary changes, and adding some targeted nutritional supplements. This type of treatment takes more time and dedication than just using a medication that treats the symptoms. However, it is well worth it in the long run and may even help prevent future health problems.

Personalized and Patient-Centered Care

Case 8: Personalized Nutritional Therapy

I have a teenage girl patient who presented with anxiety, poor nutrition, fatigue, low energy, and decreased appetite. Mom had tried different approaches to improve her diet, which were ultimately unsuccessful. She was challenging to work with, standoffish, uncommunicative, and defiant. (I know, it's hard to believe that a teenage girl would be like this, right?) She could have benefited from working with a functional medicine nutritionist, but she was unwilling and needed to be met where she was at the time and what she was willing to do. I knew that if she felt better, she could also make better choices. As she was deathly afraid of needles, bloodwork was out of the question, so we decided to do a functional medicine analysis of key nutritional biomarkers that only required her first morning urine. The results enabled us to make a plan to target nutritional therapies to meet her precise needs, and I'm happy to say that she was feeling better within a few weeks. There was still work to be done, but it was a start, and it was significantly helpful.

Gut Testing and Preventative Care

It is incredible how much information you can gain through nutritional and/or stool testing in a patient for a wide variety of presenting concerns. Without these tests, the patient might have been subjected to unnecessary prescription medications and medical interventions if an allopathic route had been chosen instead. These tests are relatively easy to do and provide invaluable information. Unfortunately, insurance companies do not see the value and usually do not pay for them. This sometimes leaves clinicians reluctant to offer them or forces families into a difficult decision, especially if they have trouble affording the out-of-pocket cost. What's ironic here is, once again, our current healthcare model's lack of emphasis on prevention within the holistic framework, which then leads to increased costs down the road when the patient is sicker.

Trusting Parental Instincts

In my career, I have noticed a recurring trend. Moms will bring their child to the doctor's office and describe the situation that they are seeking help for, and then follow it up by saying, "But I'm not a doctor" (and yes, I always want to say, "but I play one on TV," but I don't). Joking aside, I find this troubling and an indicator of the patriarchal structure of our broken healthcare system. Parents, often moms, too quickly surrender their knowledge and intuition about their child's care and needs to the ingrained cultural belief that "Doctor knows best." This can lead to a lack of trust in their own nurturing and healing abilities and, therefore, rejection of accountability.

In pediatrics and healthcare in general, I feel strongly that care should be seen as a partnership. Nobody knows more about your own or your child's wellness than you do. I know... sometimes you just need to be told what to do by someone you trust, especially when you are an over-tired, worried mom with a sick child. Healthcare providers bring their own experience, training, and education to the table, and together, you can formulate plans to increase wellness by valuing what each other has to offer. That is when true healing happens.

Case 9: Labial Adhesions—to Treat or Not to Treat?

I remember when my first daughter was just a baby, and we still lived in Minnesota. Our pediatrician diagnosed her with a labial adhesion, a common issue in infant girls that usually resolves on its own without treatment. But at the time, the mainstream recommendation was to apply estrogen-containing cream to the area to get it to open up sooner. So, my pediatrician prescribed Premarin cream (an isolate from the urine of pregnant horses) for this purpose. As I was dutifully applying it one day, it suddenly dawned on me, *Why the hell would I want to put estrogen cream on the vagina of this beautiful, perfectly healthy BABY?* Trusting my instincts, I stopped using it. When I told the doctor that I had done so at the next visit, they muttered in disagreement about my choice, but then we moved on to other topics. I left that appointment feeling slightly shamed and uncertain of my choice. Nonetheless, the adhesion opened up on its own with no issues, and that medical treatment recommendation eventually fell out of favor. *Whodathunkit.*

Case 10: Urinary Frequency and Food Sensitivities

Another instance that stands out is when my oldest daughter was having ongoing problems with urinary frequency when she was much younger. After some unsuccessful remedies, I decided to have her evaluated by my boss at the time. He ordered an ultrasound of her bladder, and in preparation, she had to drink a huge amount of fluid over the course of two hours and was instructed not to empty her bladder before the test. When we arrived at the imaging center for her scheduled appointment, she already had to urinate very badly, but they were running behind and made us wait in the waiting room. She was getting to the point of extreme discomfort—she was pale and sweaty—but they continued to make us wait. It was a very unpleasant experience for her, and the center was less than accommodating. It turned out that everything was normal. So, her doctor's only recommendation was to put her on Ditropan, which was a prescription medication for overactive bladder, most commonly prescribed for older women. She was only fifteen at the time. The laundry list of potential side effects includes "dry mouth, dizziness, drowsiness, blurred vision, dry eyes, nausea, vomiting, upset stomach, stomach pain, constipation, diarrhea, headache, unusual taste in mouth, dry/flushed skin, and weakness." Hum, no, thank you. The problem at hand didn't weigh out with the pros and cons of taking this medication.

I know the doctor was trying to help relieve her symptoms, and this was the only answer he could offer within the structure of allopathic medicine. Yet, this answer seemed counterintuitive and short-sighted, so I discussed it with my daughter, and we decided that she wouldn't take it, especially since the condition wasn't serious, debilitating, or life-threatening. The medication was also not without potential side effects. What I wanted to know was why this was happening in the first place and how I could help her without prescription medication, if possible. I decided to bring her to our Naturopathic doctor, and we also tested her for food sensitivities. She was sensitive to gluten, which was of no surprise because of our family history. At the time, it was hard to convince this teenager to change her diet and eat differently than all her friends. But when she got a little older and was having stomach pains as well, she decided on her own to try and take it out of her diet. Several symptoms resolved, including her urinary frequency. There is plenty of anecdotal evidence, as well as some older research out of Europe on "allergic bladder" with gluten exposure, and I see it frequently in my practice. Still, it is not currently accepted or acknowledged in mainstream medicine. So, unfortunately, she suffered for many years until we finally figured it out.

Practical Passionate Compassion

Patients often thank me for listening to them and for feeling like they can talk freely and openly about their concerns and choices without fear of mistreatment, dismissiveness, judgment, or coercion. Parents have happily reported that their child "has not been on antibiotics since we came to you," or "he/she was actually looking forward to seeing you today," or "he/she doesn't complain of x anymore, since doing y." I'm not saying these things to boast but to present them as they could be—the way they should be. These are the moments that help me remember why I do this, why I am deeply devoted to this, and allow me to continue even after the tough and challenging days.

Listening to my patients is actually what has taught me the most. Of course, my education and experience have been important, but the tool of really listening has proven invaluable. Listening to their stories and paying attention to their frustrations has been instrumental. I love learning about other types of care or providers who have helped them. It is just as important to listen to and validate how certain types of care have made things worse or didn't help, or stories of previous providers or family members not listening to them. Being seen, validated, and respected is potent medicine. Our divine responsibility is to be willing to hold compassion for all types of humanity, not just those who are the same or think the same. I like to think of it as "practical compassion."

Journal Prompt

Have you or a loved one experienced frustration or disappointment with the healthcare system or a particular provider? How did you handle it? Were you able to get a resolution? Have you changed the way you seek care for yourself or your loved one because of it? You might have several things to say here or just one defining moment. It could be minor or significant, or everything in between. It doesn't matter; whatever comes up is perfect.

CHAPTER 5

Navigating Turbulent Waters: Challenges, Reflections, and Hope

"Let the children's laughter remind us how we used to be."

—Lyrics from the song "The Greatest Love of All"
by Linda Creed (1977)

A couple of years into our thriving, growing practice, my partner's family was hit with a horrible, unthinkable family tragedy that threw our small, intimate office into a tailspin. Then, a few months later, I, too, was hit with a terrible, unthinkable family tragedy. It was a "you can't make this shit up" moment. Once again, the stability of our practice and our mental capacity to continue providing quality care to others was put to the test. And my understanding of integrative medicine for mind/body/spirit healing helped with these challenges.

I have a very personal, heartbreaking story to tell, even though reluctantly and with a painful amount of sadness and vulnerability. My cousin started having health problems about ten years ago. I have always been suspicious that it was a tick-borne illness, as it all started after a hiking trip in the Rocky Mountains as well as hiking all over Kentucky. However, since standard lab tests came back negative a few years into his symptoms, that possibility was dismissed. To make a long story short, he saw many different doctors and specialists through the years and was prescribed many different medications. However, his symptoms continued to worsen, and new ones emerged. Before it all started, he was young, healthy, vital, newly married, and in graduate divinity school. He and his wife were looking forward to doing missionary work when he completed his program. Even though he is about twenty years younger than me and lives in a different state, I've always had a special relationship with him and my aunt. However, as his illness and symptoms progressed, he became increasingly depressed and withdrawn. He never was able to pursue his career after finishing graduate school because of his ailing health. He ultimately became estranged from his wife, leading to their divorce.

His illness continued to progress to the point where he could barely eat and suffered from severe mental distress, constant pain, frequent vomiting, instability on his feet, and seizures. His condition was so precarious that he experienced multiple falls, resulting in several concussions and numerous trips to the ER. After three concussions in a row within a short period, he became completely disassociated and violent, leading to an unspeakable tragedy that will forever change our family. My uncle was murdered, my aunt was badly injured and severely traumatized, and my cousin is now in prison. Later on, I found out that at the time, he was on up to 27 pills a day—27! Interestingly enough, while in prison, he has been able to wean off all of his medications, is seeing a therapist monthly, following his own special diet, and is doing much better physically and mentally.

Without going into all the details over many years, I blame this horrific event on the complete failure of the medical system. I'm fully aware that when terrible things happen, it is human nature to look for somewhere to put the blame. Maybe I am doing that to some degree. But I also know that he was horribly mismanaged, misdiagnosed, and over-medicated. A few months before this tragedy, he started reaching out to me for help, and I tried the very best I could, as his mom had been trying so desperately for many years. I only wish I could have done more to help him, and I carry deep sadness and regret for that. I can only hope that by bringing some awareness and attention to the failures of our medical system, we may prevent others from experiencing such tragedy.

Lessons from the COVID-19 Pandemic

When the COVID-19 pandemic started in the winter of 2020, I was in the process of writing this book. To be honest, my writing came to an abrupt stop for over two years during that time. I had been questioning and doubting my original intentions and the purpose of the book. Also, my feelings and comprehension of the pandemic constantly evolved over the years. I didn't want to write about COVID-19, but how could I possibly write about rescuing ourselves from our current healthcare paradigm and not discuss such a significant, historical, and global health event!?

Personal and Professional Challenges

Like many, I had the challenge of handling the pandemic both on a personal and professional level. As a healthcare professional, I have navigated uncertain times while trying to give advice, guidance, and reassurance to my patients without much clarity, especially in the beginning. Patients were looking to me for answers, as I was struggling with it myself, and the available information was constantly changing, often conflicting, unclear, and seemingly distrustful.

At the beginning of the pandemic, I felt vulnerable and overwhelmed by the uncertainty of the sustainability of my business from a financial and logistical standpoint. My partner and I had to scramble to change and adjust how we operated on a daily basis to meet the heightened safety and health needs of the office and our patients. Being a small private office, we didn't have an administration or corporate office to rely on for guidance and support. On a personal level, I had to adapt our family's lifestyle and daily routines, step back from our social connections, and change how we spent our time. Additionally, I faced the challenge of supporting my teenage daughters as they dealt with feelings of isolation and fear. Most of my friends and family worked from home, but I was still going into the office to take care of patients. Because of this, I was worried people wouldn't want to be around me or my family. I was also navigating the waters of having some differences in opinion and decision-making from friends, family, and community.

Global Responses to the Pandemic

I observed how communities from all around the world were coping. Some enjoyed and marveled at the increased time at home, online communities, and the opportunity for quiet and reflection. I also watched people struggle with frustration, loss of routine and things they enjoy doing, loneliness, fear, and real financial hardship. The irony was stark—while some boasted about their Netflix-watching, takeout-ordering pajama parties, there were also the children who had relied on school for meals, socialization, and stability. Now, they were isolated at home, where the circumstances were far less supportive.

People were bitterly arguing about how to manage the quarantine and the pandemic. Conflicting arguments emerged, with some advocating to do whatever we can to protect our most vulnerable, including the immunocompromised, the elderly, as well as hospital workers. In contrast, others stressed the importance of fighting for our liberties and freedom. The government was offering us the rescue of a vaccine and the development of potential medications, but it was also fueling the fire of our polarization. But we were not a healthy society going into this, and arguing, scapegoating, and pointing fingers certainly wouldn't make anybody healthier.

Citizens and businesses received trillions of dollars in bailouts due to the economic collapse caused by the global shutdown. We are now experiencing the fallout in the form of inflation. This situation has also highlighted the profound issues within our country, which, despite being a supposed global leader, is plagued by division, hatred, bitterness, and a failing healthcare system. We could have benefited from more community efforts. The division and the separation were NOT what we need in our universal consciousness. The masking seemingly represented a metaphor to me. I believe that now, more than ever, is the time to stop hiding behind our "masks." The world needs us to speak and listen to each other. We must not be afraid of one another or avoid each other out of fear of what might be shared. We need to be open to what someone may have to share. Being fearful of one another, especially for those who are different, is an illness plaguing us. I am not saying this to disregard the importance of personal choices of how to care for themselves and their loved ones. I am just speaking allegorically. We all ultimately want the same thing: to be safe, to be loved, and to give love.

The Role of Integrative Medicine

I believe that integrative medicine has real potential to be a rising star. There is plenty of excellent research showing the powerful effects nutraceuticals can have on mitigating disease and supporting the immune system. The foundations of holistic medicine, such as healthy eating, plenty of rest, stress reduction, complementary therapies, prayer, meditation, and appropriate supplementation when needed, are more critical and valuable than ever.

In my practice, which has a large percentage of children, I am thankful that we have had very few patients who suffered from serious cases of COVID-19. We had only onc hospitalization for an infant who then fully recovered, and we have had no deaths. I feel lucky enough to say that most of our families had mild symptoms and recovered quickly. One child developed a strange reoccurring rash for a few months after the infection, but it resolved. At this point, there have been almost 1 million deaths attributed to COVID-19 in the United States. And we now have some more understanding of risk factors that make severe disease or death more likely.

Please don't mistake this conversation as suggesting that if you get COVID or had a severe case, it's because you should have just eaten healthier or taken some vitamins. That's not what I'm saying at all. Despite doing my best to take care of my physical and emotional health, I believe I had COVID-19 in January 2020 (before testing was available) and was sick for several weeks. I had it again in the summers of 2022 and 2023. While I felt ill for several days each time, I'm grateful to have recovered fully without the need for hospitalization or medication.

There continue to be many things we do not understand about this virus and this disease. And as I have tried to express in different ways, the continuum of health/wellness and disease is multifactorial. What is glaringly lacking, however, is accessibility. The disease has disparately affected those living in poverty, especially African-American and Hispanic communities. Health and wellness should never be reserved for the wealthy or a particular race or culture.

Redefining the Healthcare Conversation

I have watched the mainstream media and conversations focus primarily on beating the virus with the vaccine or medications. We are repeatedly told to "follow the science." Western medicine traditionally takes this approach, and don't get me wrong, this is a very important conversation to be had. The research into how to treat a novel virus is necessary. We need "science" that asks some different questions, and we need some different methodologies. Do we really want the leaders who got us here in the first place to be the only ones making decisions on how to get us out of it? What is glaringly lacking to me is the conversation about the "host," or the person who carries the disease. A virus cannot cause disease without a host. Therefore, it is crucial to discuss how to best support the host/person to reduce the likelihood of getting sick, lessen the severity of the disease, and minimize transmission. Wearing masks, isolation, and washing your hands is an important part of the conversation, but it should not stop there. That is where integrative or functional medicine can step in.

Unfortunately, the two sides don't seem to be communicating on a national level or coming together for the greater good. Some holistic practitioners who have spoken of this have been slandered and bullied. One would think that something simple like recommending Vitamin D was god-forsaken heresy, for crying out loud! On a small scale, in my integrative office in central Connecticut, my partner and I have been able to help support our families successfully through COVID-19 and "COVID-like" (without a positive test) illnesses. Admittedly, we tend to have a healthier and younger population, which will skew our outcomes.

We know that co-morbidities like diabetes and obesity increase the severity of COVID-19 infections. This is our chance to take a look at our overall health and healthcare industry as Americans. We need to recognize where we have great strengths, advancements, and advantages, balanced with where we need to shift our focus and what changes need to be made. My hope for the future of our healthcare system is less profit-driven influence by the trillion-dollar pharmaceutical companies as well as the food and agriculture industries. I wish for a nation where the money and corporate lobbyists would get out of politics, where our politicians remember who they actually work for, where we can rebuild trust, and

return to focusing on "we the people, for the people." We need all of us because we are all in this together.

Navigating a World of (Mis)information and Manipulation

My dear friend and colleague Dr. Miela Gruber shared this provocative statement in a brilliant social media post:

"There's a lot of people out there who are pissed off that 'science' and the words 'I believe in science' are being levied as a weapon at them. Maybe they just aren't used to it since they aren't the usual target for that phrase. The unfortunate historical meaning of that kind of manipulation of the word science is really, 'The only real science is a specific science that props up a specific paradigm for specific people and a specific economic system.' 'Science,' like religion and education, can be weaponized, and we all need to be aware and careful of that. That phrase and even science itself have been used as a racialized weapon of colonialism and capitalism for a long time. If someone recently used that phrase to dismiss you, and you were shocked, then it's time you learned about how science was used to construct whiteness, and dismiss anyone non-European, their medicine, farming, customs, and knowledge, as 'nonscientific'. 'Not Science' has sometimes been code for not European, not white, or not in line with economic growth. Science is only unbiased on the most surface level because it is only capable of answering the questions people choose to ask, and the questions are bound by their culture, as is the methodology. I am not bashing science—as someone who finds biochemistry super sexy, believe me, I am not. But we need to understand it in context."

Sadly, our society has gotten used to being manipulated and lied to. Occasionally, we hear of the people who were caught and found accountable. Yet sometimes, it feels as though they are only the "sacrificial lambs." Politicians, celebrities, big Agriculture, big Pharma, corporations, social media moguls… the list goes on. We don't know who to believe anymore. People often align themselves with a particular side to feel safe, then label the other side as the offenders, the enemies, or the ones causing the problem. Democrats vs. Republicans. Liberal vs. Conservative. Corporations vs. the people. The elite vs. the working class. Religion, culture, and race wars. The

1% vs. all of us. This way, you can blame someone else instead of taking any accountability or responsibility. At least you don't have to constantly feel confused, weeding through the muck of conflicting information and making your own decisions. There is so much misinformation on both sides of these "arguments." This applies to everything, including politics, cultures, religions, economics, morality, health, and body autonomy. The world is heartbreaking right now, and innocent people and children are being affected. Our human nature is to want to belong, feel supported, and be part of a tribe, so we will often choose one side and blindly stick to the narrative to feel safe and accepted. It is much harder to remain in the middle, knowing that the truth lies somewhere in between but constantly struggling to find it. The two sides will yell at each other, neither hearing the other nor contributing to any change and awareness. Ironically, they will often argue the same points but with different spins. An example of this is the tagline, "not fear-based, but science-based." People love to use this line to attack each other on both sides of the aisle, so much to the point that the meaning of the "slogan" has become lost and invalid. Any good scientist will readily admit that there is a lot that we don't know that even science can't explain, that science is ever-evolving, and yes, even science makes mistakes.

What is labeled "misinformation" today may be "truth" tomorrow or vice versa. There are countless examples of this throughout our history. We need to learn how to have these complex and challenging conversations with respect and open minds. The right to question is the cornerstone of scientific exploration. I often find myself in the middle, seeing validity in various points and conversations while recognizing that one's ultimate truth is affected by many influencing factors. One's ultimate truth can be found within if you can be quiet enough to hear it. But it's harder there, and it feels lonely. Sometimes, it feels compelling just to pick a side and stand more confidently in those convictions because at least you know that you will have a family, support, and others who feel the same. But we can't always do that, so we continue to weed through the muck of conflicting information, lies, and manipulation. At these times, I try to breathe through the unknowing and root down into who I am, why I am here, and how I serve. Then, I more clearly know how to make choices and how to speak my truth. I am constantly striving to balance staying informed about current events through various news sources with protecting myself from feeling overwhelmed and fearful, which can be counterproductive. This balance lies somewhere between naivety and toxicity and is not always easy to achieve. However, it is essential to find this equilibrium.

Nurturing Trust, Empowering Patients, and Embracing Holistic Healthcare

One of the most important hallmarks of holistic medicine and the future of healthcare is the client-provider relationship, characterized by trust, open communication, and the lack of bias. I understand the desire to trust authorities, doctors, and governing bodies. Most people prefer guidance in areas they don't feel particularly knowledgeable about. Sometimes, you just need someone to say, "Don't worry, I got this; you can trust me. I'll take care of you."

Unfortunately, we can't always have blind faith in our healthcare industry, which I believe is failing miserably in many areas. And we certainly can't always have blind trust in Google, which is also being censored and controlled. At times, the burden falls on the individual to engage in critical thinking and deep inner investigation. There is a wealth of information available on the internet at the drop of a dime, but you must be a conscious consumer. Information can be overwhelming and misleading at times. Anything can be construed to serve an agenda, including statistics. Just because there is "data" to support something doesn't mean it can't be misconstrued.

Unfortunately, pharmaceutical companies are often the only corporations with the funds to do the desired randomized controlled trials, which are considered the gold standard of research. Yet pharmaceutical companies may not be addressing the questions some of us ask. It is always preferable to use evidence-based medicine, but scientific inquiry and decision-making should also include critical thinking, clinical observation, and collective observation. We must keep asking questions, staying curious, and open to possibilities.

Now, Artificial Intelligence is infiltrating our information systems. However, AI lacks a heart. Our society reveres left-brain intelligence and intellect, so much so that we have lost capacity in the more nuanced, yet very important world of creativity, imagination, mystery, wonder and intuition. F. Scott Fitzgerald is well known for saying, "The test for first-rate intelligence is the ability to hold two opposed ideas and still retain the ability to function." I believe having open, nuanced, and honest conversations with your child's healthcare provider is vital to talk through complex issues and navigate these ever-evolving times.

Parents should never feel harassed or bullied for their questions or decisions. There is always a way to have respectful dialogue. I was recently conversing with a mom about ordering a possible test for her child, and she said to me in appreciation, "I'm not used to having conversations based on common sense instead of just going by the usual procedures." It makes me cringe when I hear stories from families about their experiences with previous pediatricians and healthcare providers. It is not uncommon to hear how they felt uncomfortable with choices and decisions that they felt were forced upon them or how they were not listened to or treated disrespectfully. This is shame-worthy for a profession that is supposed to be care providers. Even in hospitals during childbirth, when moms are at their most vulnerable—sleep-deprived, hormonal, and ferociously desperate to make the best choices for their precious newborn—they find themselves in unfamiliar territory. No mother should feel belittled, shamed, or bullied when she is in the hospital with her newborn, at their first pediatrician appointment, or at any other time. There is always a way to discuss important health decisions without mistreating the patient. Maternal instinct, connectedness, and knowledge should never be diminished by the patriarchal construct. When I say "patriarchy," I want to be clear here that I am not singling out men; I am speaking of an ingrained oppressive operating system in which we all participate, knowingly or unknowingly.

The first time I was pregnant, though I didn't know it yet, I went to the store to get a pregnancy test because my cycle was late, and my husband and I had just started trying to conceive. When I got home from the store, I felt particularly tired, so I laid down and closed my eyes for a moment. When my eyes opened, still in the hazy period between sleep and awakening, I saw a brief vision above me and coming towards me—a beautiful, nurturing, woman's face surrounded by white light. I knew within every cell of my body that I was pregnant and had been given the gift and blessing of motherhood. The next morning, I took the pregnancy test, and of course, it was positive. I had felt from a deep level how motherhood is divine and sacred. This should always be recognized and nurtured, never belittled.

Teaching Health from an Early Age

I feel so blessed to work with children and their families. The impact of establishing great health habits and a relationship to wellness as a young child carries lifelong rewards. An integrative and holistic approach to care from early on has a significant positive influence on reducing disease and influencing long-term health outcomes. I also believe that it's vital for children to develop positive early relationships with their pediatricians and healthcare providers. This provides them with a framework for expectations, a foundation of trust, knowledge on navigating the healthcare system as they grow older, and the understanding that it is a collaborative partnership.

In the textbook *The Fundamentals of Complementary and Alternative Medicine,* I adore Micozzi's definition of wellness as "a focus on engaging the inner resources of each individual as an active and conscious participant in the maintenance of his or her own health." I believe strongly in the importance of maintenance and prevention as opposed to the current medicalization of "fixing the problem." Starting young, we should teach our children the fundamentals of health, including aspects like diet, sleep, exercise, mindfulness, and joy.

Isn't it better to learn practices like meditation, energy healing, exercise, spending time in nature, and good nutrition early on? This way, you can avoid downplaying these aspects and perhaps reduce the chances of severe anxiety, autoimmune diseases, or other health issues later in life when stress becomes overwhelming.

We do have a lot to be grateful for in our healthcare systems, particularly the frontline providers who offer cutting-edge, life-saving medications and interventions. Western medicine has made incredible advances in these areas. As I am writing this in the era of the COVID-19 pandemic, I am honored to be among the class of "essential healthcare workers" and have great respect and admiration for all the nurses, doctors, and healthcare providers working with dedication in the ER's, urgent cares, hospitals and ICU's, despite the emotional and physical toll.

Yet Western medicine's sole focus on killing this bug, removing that bad thing, stopping these symptoms—doesn't resonate with me... at least not all the time. However, in this current world, where polarization is seemingly worse than ever, I feel a powerful call to drop the arms and work together. Both allopathic and holistic healthcare are valuable and meaningful. We don't have to "throw the baby out with the bath water." There is power in using both, depending on what is needed. Both ways deserve respect. This is what integrative medicine truly is. I believe in the body's innate ability to heal with nurturing and listening. I am also a curious, open scientist who is always willing to learn and consider new perspectives. I extend this encouragement to everyone.

Journal Prompt

What do you like the best about your life right now? What do you wish you could change? What challenges have you faced that you feel have significantly shaped you? What are you grateful for? You might have several things to say here or just one relevant thing to you. It could be minor or significant, or everything in between; it doesn't matter; whatever comes up is perfect.

CHAPTER 6

Hope for Our Future: Stepping Out of Line

"Find Your Strength in Love."

—Lyrics from the song "The Greatest Love of All"
by Linda Creed (1977)

I love what I do and am excited and honored to share my journey with you in the hopes that it will inspire, ignite, inform, and transform. Or, at the least, make you ponder and question. I am dedicated to bringing some heart and hope back into medicine, health, and healing. Consumers are looking for it, and practitioners realize there can be a better way. However, it would be short-sighted not to address integrative medicine's issues, challenges, and limitations, along with some ideas for the sustainability of this type of healthcare for our future.

Addressing Burnout

Burnout and compassion fatigue are pressing issues for care providers of all kinds. It is disheartening to watch the downward spiral of healthcare. There is generally very little support or conversation around self-care for healthcare providers. How can we truly help others if we can't even help ourselves? I have had several discussions over the last several years with many types of healthcare providers about how it feels that the needs and challenges of patients are greater and more complex than ever. On top of that, the frustrations with the healthcare system from providers and patients are higher than ever. I am happy to see that this issue is becoming a bit more of the conversation, especially among the younger generations starting their education and careers. One of the biggest challenges for integrative providers is avoiding burnout while also feeling empowered to take care of their own needs alongside those of others.

We do not need to sacrifice ourselves. We do not need to be martyrs. In fact, it's the opposite. You can still be empathetic while maintaining healthy boundaries. We can empathize with others while still shielding ourselves from harm. I have learned the hard way how important it is to "give from a full cup."

There is not just one right way for someone to nourish themselves. My morning and evening practices are an essential part of my day, no matter what is going on. Meditation, prayer, journaling, gratitude practice, exercise, dance, getting outside, and anything that brings you joy are all incredible tools to stay grounded and connected. When you have less time, just take a few minutes for something that is most important to you. At other times, when possible, take more time for these practices. The truth is that when we nurture our well-being, we are also role modeling for our children the value of self-care, taking time to replenish our spirit, and living a balanced life, therefore benefiting them as well.

One of my favorite things to do every morning when I first wake up, even before getting out of bed, is to be grateful for a few things in my life. This can take just a minute. It can be very simple, like being grateful for your warm bed, the sunrise, or even for waking up to a new day. Or you can be more specific about the people and/or things in your life if you choose.

In the warmer months, I love starting my mornings by putting my bare feet on the ground for a few minutes, a practice of "grounding", also known as "earthing", by standing in the grass before heading off to work or starting my day. While grounding and its health benefits have existed for thousands of years, a growing body of research is supportive of the positive physiological effects of restoring an electrical connection with the earth.

Meditation is also a powerful tool to promote emotional and physical health and well-being. In the appendix at the end of this book, I offer you a walking meditation that I developed several years ago and the reasons for why it has been one of my cherished tools for reconnection and self-nourishment.

Addressing Fair Compensation

Another challenge for integrative healthcare providers is getting adequately reimbursed for the work we are so passionate about. Integrative/holistic medicine inherently takes more time than the traditional allopathic delivery of healthcare. If your business takes insurance, providers need to consider that they might not even get paid for certain visits because of all the hoops that need to be jumped through to be reimbursed by healthcare insurance carriers. A significant problem that I see from having a health insurance system is that it separates the care and service given with the value and the cost understood by the consumer with a third-party payer. Revenue is lost because of time and resources spent tracking claims, resubmitting, handling problems, and ensuring that patients follow through on their responsibilities for managing their insurance carriers. This system also creates one of the few professions that provide service, who not only have to wait but also often have to fight to get reimbursed for the service already provided to the client. This causes revenue to be lost from time spent by either the clinician or the staff, as well as resources used. Often, the reimbursement is already lower than it should be, especially for primary care providers. Healthcare insurance companies often do not provide a "raise" or increase in pay for solo or small practice providers who do not have the resources or staffing to meet the "medical home" and "productivity" criteria to increase reimbursement, even though other costs of running a medical business increase with inflation over time, just like everywhere else.

Health insurance carriers will often deny paying for claims for no other reason than, well, that they can get away with it. They continue to come up with new, made-up reasons to deny claims, which continually confuses offices and billing staff. And now one major carrier has taken it upon themselves to actually change submitted billing codes to be able to reimburse less than the contracted rate. When providers "contract" with a health insurance provider, they have to accept the payment that the carrier is willing to pay them, no matter what, with no questions asked and no other recourse. For example, if a service is decidedly worth $175, but the patient's insurance carrier says it will only pay you $78, then $78 is all you will get, regardless of the excellent, thorough, or complex care you give them.

Our current healthcare system is moving fast towards large-scale, production-line medicine, if not already there. Many doctors who once worked independently or in small groups are jumping ship quickly because of the ever-increasing challenges and joining this black hole of Big Medicine. The tagline is often boasted to save money, time, and resources. Still, some providers see the slippery slope, as I do, that this pursuit of size and market power will lead to raising prices instead of lowering them, as well as reducing quality, if our past has taught us anything. Unfortunately, I do not believe Big Medicine will serve the greater social good, just like with Big Pharma and Big Agriculture.

The health insurance industry does not value time spent with patients, which is needed to address root causes and take a holistic approach. Medical offices that do well within the health insurance model need to see a large volume of patients daily, meaning they need to spend less time with each patient to be financially successful. This is a one-size-fits-all type of healthcare. An algorithm needs to be created to do this effectively, and each individual is treated accordingly. This has proven successful for chain restaurants and chain stores. Algorithms and rigid procedures can be highly effective in certain industries that don't deal with human bodies and diseases. However, we are too individual for this approach to work well for everyone all the time. Consumers are becoming increasingly disinterested in this method, especially as they witness its repeated failures.

In the meantime, integrative providers are faced with decisions about how many patients they can serve, how much time they can spend, and if they can actually afford to take insurance at all in order to stay open and be sustainable. Many providers who value the time spent with their patients choose to run a cash-based practice where patients directly pay for their services or a concierge or membership-type projection of what they will receive and what it will include. Most seasoned providers with recognition in their communities will do this to be appropriately reimbursed, knowing all too well that it is the best way to ensure sustainability and growth.

However, cash payment is not an option for many families, and providers are challenged by not wanting only to serve the wealthy and upper class. Another option is to take insurance and also charge a smaller membership fee to offset the costs of running an integrative office that insurance does not cover, like longer appointment times, smaller, more intimate offices, and a more individualized approach. This keeps care more affordable for clients who already have to pay monthly premiums for their health insurance plans. This is what my practice has chosen to do to remain more accessible, as well as sustainable, while also having other options for families who truly can't afford it at all.

For a change to occur, consumers have to demand it. I hope that in the future, health insurance plans will reimburse their contracted providers in a way that is sustainable and fair so that extra costs don't need to be put on the consumer who chooses alternative approaches. But right now, health insurance carriers have too much power, as well as too much money. Somehow, this needs to change and be controlled, even though it feels insurmountable.

Any provider you talk to would be able to roll their eyes or concur about stories of where the insurance dictated the type of care the patient received. Which often can make it harder for us to do our job at the least, or in the worst cases, lead to total abandonment of the clinical profession. One typical example is the loophole in the "prior authorization" process for a prescribed medication or procedure. This just ends up wasting time and resources and delaying care. Obviously, the provider has "authorized" it if they ordered or prescribed it in the first place, right? Is anyone with me on this one? We've all come across heartbreaking news stories of individuals unable to afford their medication, forced to ration it, or families resorting to fundraising campaigns or taking out second mortgages to cover their child's medical expenses. Some have even tragically passed away while waiting for insurance to authorize necessary healthcare. It's utterly heartbreaking, unacceptable, and sickening.

We Need to Do Better

My mother recently had a horrible experience during an emergency room visit at our local hospital. She had fallen out of her wheelchair at home, and, unfortunately, when she landed, she hit her face. When the EMT personnel came to help her back into her chair, since there was a fair amount of blood, they insisted that she go to the hospital, even though she did not want to. When she arrived, the ER was overcrowded and understaffed, with no available beds. At first, they put her in a little alcove, but at least a small curtain could be drawn. They did an X-ray and said that she had broken her nose but didn't advise anything else except to make an appointment to see a specialist. However, one of the doctors became concerned about the ulcer on her foot, even though it was unrelated to why she was there. She was being treated for chronic cellulitis by several doctors for quite some time. Still, because of the peripheral neuropathy and her MS, it was an ongoing and complicated problem. The ER doctors told her she needed multiple rounds of IV antibiotics and refused to discharge her, even though she asked to go home and receive care from her own doctors who knew her history. She was then moved out to the hallway and left to sleep under the bright lights all night. She actually had to beg to get some water. Finally, a secretary who felt terrible for her got up from her desk to bring her some.

The next day, when she was still reluctant to get the IV antibiotics, they began to bully and coerce her. They made her feel stupid and small. One of the doctors even used emotional manipulation and told her, "If you were my mother, I would make sure you did this." My mother asked them to consult with her doctors, but they did not. What they didn't know about my mother and were unwilling to listen to was that she is extremely sensitive to medications and can only handle tiny doses, and even then, she would still have adverse reactions and side effects. But they would not listen to her, and she was manipulated to do the IV antibiotics against her will. After she was finally discharged three days later, she was very sick for a month with severe diarrhea and could not eat much of anything. Her digestive system was never the same after all those antibiotics. She developed many new food allergies, restricting her diet even more, and she lost a lot of weight that she couldn't afford to lose. To make matters worse, the ER treatment had no positive effect on the issue with her foot.

My mother talks about the horrors she witnessed in the ER those nights—overcrowding and under-staffing, patients moaning and groaning and not getting care fast enough. There were not enough beds for everyone. Despite that, she was still forced to stay there against her will and better judgment. Nurses were running around like crazy trying to keep up and doing their best, but in impossible situations. You would think these were circumstances that only happened in developing countries. Not the case.

How to Do Better

So, what is the better proposition for the future of our healthcare industry? One that controls costs as well as quality? One that ensures better outcomes and, therefore, reduced burden and reduced costs? In hospital settings, it is imperative that we place importance on better nursing staff ratios. Doctors' egos should never be a part of healthcare decision-making. Nobody should be forced into medical interventions against their will. For outpatient settings, I know I have spoken quite a bit about providers needing more time to provide quality care. But how can this time be reimbursed? Especially when health insurance carriers place little value on time spent with patients. I'm open to the conversation here because I will admit that it is not my expertise. But I do know that we need massive health care reform. To start, I hope that health insurance carriers will realize the value of integrative, holistic medicine and begin to cover these services better. There also needs to be more value placed on time spent with the patient and provider, as well as the provider-patient relationship in general. Placing value on this model should reduce costs and burden on the healthcare industry as patients remain healthier as they age. Big Pharma may not like this. Big Medicine may not like this. They do not stand to make as much money if we are all healthier. What we currently have is sick-care, not healthcare. Does this proposition for change ultimately look like socialized medicine? Not necessarily, but perhaps there is room for discussion.

I strongly believe that the influence of holistic medicine is most powerful when you begin this type of care in infancy or childhood. I also feel that if patients had better relationships and trust in their primary care providers, it could lessen the cost and burden on our emergency rooms and urgent care clinics, where care is more expensive.

I hope to bring more discussion into the patriarchal, culturally ingrained idea of the indoctrinated "doctor knows best." I have always felt the importance of meeting patients where they are, which means seeing them as a whole person with their own expectations, experiences, past traumas, beliefs, and fears. All these things are valid and should be respected and valued, with room for open, honest discussions. Bullying, coercion, and manipulation should never be a part of healthcare decision-making.

Everyone Doing Their Part

We are all faced with many horrible issues and challenges in our world today. War, poverty, discrimination, abuse of power, destruction of our earth, unsustainability, animal cruelty, violence, trafficking, greed, and inequality. At times, it can feel hopeless, overwhelming, and devastating. Fortunately, we also have many champions and incredible humans working towards change and addressing these issues. I was a young child of the 1970s and a big "Mister Rogers" fan. I still remember how he talked about his mother saying, "Look for the helpers" in times of tragedy or upsetting news, as it left a big impression on me. These "helpers" are inspiring and leading the way, dedicated to their mission and fearless truth-telling. I wish I could help with all of these causes, but at least I know there is one way I can contribute towards the health and wellness of our children and our future. I now see my path as a member of the growing pioneer movement for the future of our healthcare industry, contributing to the health and well-being of children so they can reach their highest potential and become who they are meant to be in the world. Einstein said we wouldn't solve our problems from the level of thinking that created them. It's time for change. We need to look at things differently. We need to do better. And I know we can.

My Heartfelt, Vulnerable, and Authentic Offerings

As I am writing this, I have a successful, busy integrative practice, and I feel blessed and full of gratitude for all of the support from my loved ones and colleagues along the way. Yet, it has been full of trials and tribulations, blood, sweat, tears, and many curve balls. Some days, I feel disheartened. On other days, I remember that I have always wanted this, didn't think I could ever have it, and have worked very hard for it. I feel aligned with my divine purpose on those days and am truly grateful. Some days, I am full of righteous rage and disgust, coupled with complete disheartenment towards the healthcare industry, the health insurance industry, and the pharmaceutical industry, as well as resulting entitlements from consumers. On other days, I am filled with love for my patients and what I can offer them. I get to feel all the joy and all the suffering. Our mistakes and challenging experiences lead us to where we are now and how we want to move forward in this world. The more I feel, the more I grow. As we gain deeper gratitude for our challenges, we shift from victim to participant and student. My growth and evolution as a person and healthcare provider is not despite all the challenges, but because of it. I wouldn't have it any other way.

As I am now freshly past the sacrificial time of having young children at home and entering into a new phase of "empty nester" and menopause, I find that my focus, desires, truths, and passions are evolving and expanding. I am more prepared to share, speak, and let my truth and authenticity be seen in a whole new way. I have matured from a young rebel who saw a problem to a committed leader for the long haul. Bucking against a broken system doesn't always work; what we really need is devotion filled with love, wisdom, and vision. It is the way of the divine feminine.

As I reflect on the delicate balance between feelings of worthlessness and vanity, I am struck knowing that we are all a part of the bigger picture. It is not just "me" who is special for what I offer; we all have natural talents and innate gifts to bring forth into this world. Pediatric care is a way that I know I can contribute. As parents and healthcare providers for children, we get to support them in their physical, mental, and spiritual journeys, to awaken and invite them to express their inner genius and unique spirit. And that is such a gift and a blessing. There is a lot of despair and struggle in this world, and many problems urgently need attention. We need all of us, and we need all of us in this together.

As I enter another turning point in my career, I am faced again with the challenges of impending burnout and abandoning myself. I balance it with continued self-nurturing, inner-knowing, and my services. I am running a business and providing care to patients while continuing to find ways to support myself as I give the care and service that I know is my soul's purpose. I am working to create something sustainable, replicable, productive, and nourishing.

It is shocking and heartbreaking to look at the statistics around burnout, abandonment, and even suicide among healthcare providers. We must constantly refocus and work to become the master of our own energy and vitality so that we can serve others more effectively and support providers of all kinds to do the same. Healthcare providers are only human and need nourishing, healing, and sustaining, too. I revere the motto, "Healers heal thyself." This includes caregivers and parents, of course!

Sometimes, I feel I am failing in this area, and sometimes, I do quite well, but either way, it is important to me to "walk the talk" and lead by example. It is common for care providers and healers to struggle with creating boundaries and honoring themselves and their professional knowledge and skills as valuable. There is a fine line between doing whatever you can to help another in need and abandoning your sovereignty. I bring forth a protocol for healthcare providers as well as other leaders and coaches:

- Do not be afraid to have boundaries. As caregivers, it can feel like going "against your grain." But it is essential to know your own limits within a loving construct, or you will be at risk of burnout, growing bitter, and being no good to anyone!
- There is nothing shameful in charging for the value of your services and time. You are worth it! Money is an exchange of energy, and if you constantly devalue your services, it will ultimately reduce the quality of your care.
- Take time off and do things that you love. Nurture yourself regularly. To be healthy, vital, and whole in the best way possible is one of the greatest things you can do for your patients and families. Embody your leadership and service. Revere the motto "my cup runneth over" and give from a place of nourishment, as you cannot provide as well when you are depleted.
- Be easy on yourself. You may have mishaps or slip-ups in all these areas. We are only human. With love in our hearts, willingness to learn, and remaining curious and open, there are really no mistakes.
- We must hold ourselves gently while we work through our anger, frustrations, and pain, as we would with our children. Transmute your sense of outrage to give it power and usefulness! Become a sacred disruptor and truth-teller with your Fierce Compassion.
- When you lose sight of your vision and feel stressed, overwhelmed, sad, or angry, gently remind yourself, *yes, these feelings are valid, yet, what a gift it is to be able to serve others in the way of the healer.*

This is the story that I have chosen to impart to you. I am dedicated to healing the healthcare institution from the inside out. I shared my journey, wisdom, failures, and achievements with you. Even if I am only one drop in the ripple effect of revolutionizing our healthcare industry, I know I have contributed to the future of our children. I hope to have planted seeds of change and points of transformation, but most of all, love.

"Alchemy"*—seemingly magical process of transformation, creation, or combination*

Journal prompt

What do you feel are your gifts and talents? Do you have a divine mission or purpose in this life? Are you trying to figure out what that is? What can you do to support yourself to do this most effectively? You might have several things to say here or just one relevant thing. It could be minor or significant, or everything in between. It doesn't matter; whatever comes up is perfect.

Appendix A: What Now?

Thank you for making it all the way through this book with me! We are in this together. Are you wondering what to do next? You can journal or ponder on these questions. These are intended to help you take actions and steps for better healthcare.

Are you a mom? Wondering about ways to find better care for your child?

1. Search for holistic and/or integrative pediatrics in your area.
2. Talk to other like-minded moms about how to support each other and where they seek care.
3. Find a provider who listens to you with respect and does not make you feel pressured or uncomfortable.
4. Don't wait for your annual wellness exam to raise other concerns you may have. Schedule a separate appointment to ensure your provider has adequate time and attention to address these issues thoroughly. This helps avoid feeling rushed and unheard while respecting both your and your provider's need for sufficient time and attention.
5. If you would like to propose/discuss a different type of care, option, or management that your provider has recommended, I would also suggest you make a separate appointment to do so.
6. If you are not getting what you need, be brave and ask for it.
7. Understand that your provider is only human and may have limitations in their role. Approach with mutual respect. "Do unto others as you would have done unto you." You ultimately both want what's best for your child. If that's not the case, then find care elsewhere.

Are you a healthcare provider interested in transitioning to a more holistic/integrative approach?

1. Search for local or online programs, classes, and seminars in your areas of interest.
2. Follow the online blogs/posts of the types of providers that you admire.
3. Get out and introduce yourself/network with other providers in similar fields. Send an email or letter expressing your interest.
4. Start asking your patients what type of care they would be interested in if they had options.
5. Start asking your patients about their frustrations with their medical care.
6. Contemplate what you love about your current job and what you would like to change.
7. Commit to your self-care practices to be as healthy and whole as possible when caring for others. There is no one right way to do this. Whatever feeds your soul and brings you joy.

Appendix B: My Favorite Walking Meditation

My offering to you...

Let's face it: our lives are very full. We have unending to-do lists. We multi-task well. Adding meditation practices radically improves our ability to cope and thrive with all our responsibilities.

The Power of Meditation and Mindfulness

For thousands of years, meditation has been practiced by seekers of higher consciousness. For us, in this modern day, it is medicine for alleviating stress, managing emotions, decreasing anxiety and depression, and guiding us in good decision-making. It has physical, mental, and emotional benefits.

As babies, we live in the present moment; you can witness this in your own children. Our indoctrination into culture trained us to dwell in the past, worry about the future, and abandon the most important aspect of our essence: present-moment consciousness. It is there that we find joy, freedom, and peace. As a practice, meditation retrains our brain waves to restrengthen our connection with the present moment. When we have this experience, even briefly, we feel alive and clear.

Several years ago, a groundbreaking study was published in *Biological Psychiatry.* The research used the Western model of scientific thoroughness to study mindfulness meditation. The impressive results showed that meditation could change the brains of ordinary people and potentially improve their health.

Meditation and mindfulness have numerous well-researched and documented health benefits. The benefits of meditation can touch many areas of your life as you become more present and attentive with your children, family, loved ones, clients, and yourself! Meditation can be done anywhere, anytime, and is free!

Simply put, it is a vehicle toward a better life.

Walking Meditation

Walking meditation is a form of meditation in action. For some people, it is easier to be more aware of their bodies while doing walking meditation than sitting meditation. It is a simple tool to help us appreciate our experience. It can make walking a more intense experience as well as very enjoyable. It is easy to practice and enhances physical, mental, emotional, and spiritual well-being.

Common Misconceptions

It is a misconception that the only way to meditate is by sitting. What is most important is what is happening internally and not how you look from the outside. Therefore, it doesn't matter if you are in a pretty "lotus position" or not. We have all seen the yoga models on magazine covers assuming this classic position. We often feel that if we don't have the perfect meditation cushion, beautiful candle, or peaceful area to meditate, we are not doing it right or achieving the goal. We have all heard someone say that they "just can't sit still" to meditate or just can't fit it into their day.

It is a misconception that walking meditation is a more novice form. Walking meditation is a great way to incorporate meditation into our ordinary lives because you can do it anytime you walk! This includes normal circumstances like walking from your office to your car. In walking meditation, you use the physical, mental, and emotional experience of walking to develop greater awareness.

There are several different styles of walking meditation. What follows is the meditation I have adopted as my own. You can find beautiful, guided walking meditations online, in libraries, and in bookstores. The ever-inspiring meditation teacher, Thich Nhat Hahn, has published numerous discussions about walking meditation, including his book *Peace is Every Step: The Path of Mindfulness in Everyday Life.*

In 1979, Jon Kabat-Zinn introduced an eight-week stress reduction program. Now, 37 years later, Mindfulness-Based Stress Reduction (MBSR) has entered the mainstream of healthcare and scientific study. Kabat-Zinn speaks of walking meditation in one of my favorite books, *Wherever You Go, There You Are.*

There are differences between walking meditation and sitting meditation, especially since you must keep your eyes open so you won't trip or bump into something or someone! Therefore, you don't withdraw your attention from the outside world like you might do with sitting meditation at home.

There are no rights or wrongs with where or for how long you will do it. However, I suggest finding a route with less traffic, like a quiet neighborhood or park. Walking by water or in the woods is ideal if you have the option. I would carve out at least twenty minutes if possible.

The Reason

As a parent or caregiver, you are often so busy caring for everyone else that you usually put yourself last on the list. Since others rely so heavily on you, it is essential to remember to take care of yourself. A survey from the American Psychological Association shows that women are more likely than men to experience physical and emotional symptoms of stress. Children are sensitive to their mother's stress and reportedly have higher stress levels when their moms are overworked, anxious, or depressed. It is well-documented that stress has numerous adverse health consequences. It is ideal for busy moms to have several tools they can access to help alleviate stress and its unhealthy consequences. Healthy eating and sleeping habits are on the top of the list. But just as important are ways to add more joy, fun, and conscious awareness.

Ever since my children were young, one of my favorite things to do when I have a small amount of free time is to go for a walk. If they were napping or if I had another person at home to watch them, I would often choose to get out of the house and just walk. My intent was to clear my mind and get some exercise so that after I returned, I was better equipped to handle the rest of the day. But what I often found instead was that as I attacked that walk with fervor, my racing mind would ruminate about my current stresses and problems. I would ruminate about how mad I was at my husband, beat myself up about how I overreacted to my child's behaviors, worry about money… you get the drift. When I returned to the house, I wasn't in a better place. In fact, I was in the same mood, if not worse, as when I left. I would feel frustrated that I didn't feel any better, and I just "fed fuel to the fire" of my stress. Over time, I finally admitted to myself that this wasn't healthy for anyone involved.

For many years, I have been on a wonderful journey of exploring, incorporating, and discovering holistic health and mind-body healing. Being a healthcare provider has greatly enriched my work with my patients, as well as my family and myself. Several years back, I developed a walking meditation that never fails to give me a blast of much-needed tranquility and clarity. I call it "Two for One" because you get exercise and mindfulness simultaneously! You also get much-needed time in nature and time alone with yourself. It has spiritual and physical benefits. It is relatively quick and simple. You can spend fifteen minutes, or you can spend an hour or more. This meditation came to me intuitively and was greatly influenced by my meditation studies over the last several years and its profound effects.

The Walking Meditation

When I first set out, I allow myself to have my thoughts for several minutes, or however long it takes. As I walk, I imagine these thoughts or circumstances blowing off my back behind me while I leave them behind as I continue to walk forward. When I am ready, I begin consciously and deliberately going through the following concepts, one at a time: Seeing, Hearing, Smelling, Feeling, and Experiencing. As I am mindful of one sense, I block out the others so that I can be fully present with each one.

1. **Seeing:** Close off all your other senses, look around, and really take in your environment through your eyes. Look at the color of the sky and the shape of the clouds. Look at buildings, trees, or the landscape. Look at people, animals, or cars that you pass. Look at the road, grass, or land you are walking on. Whatever is in your environment, look at it without judgment, analysis, or decision-making. Simply look.

2. **Hearing**: Just listen to whatever it is that you hear. It could be the wind or the rustling of the trees. It could be the honking of the cars, church bells, or the noise of traffic going by. It could be people talking or the noise of construction. It might be the sounds of your footsteps on the chosen terrain. Just listen without judgment, analysis, or decision-making.
3. **Smelling**: Smell the earthy smells or the city smells. The smell of hot, steamy pavement or the smell of crisp, cool air. The scent of what is cooking in the house you are walking by or the smell of the pavement being poured at the construction site. The smell of the ocean or the garbage from the garbage bins. Just smell the surroundings, no judgment, just smell.
4. **Feeling *physically***: Feel the temperature on your skin. Feel the sun or lack thereof. Feel the humidity or the dryness. Feel the precipitation. Feel the wind against you as you walk forward. No judgments, just feel.
5. **Feeling *emotionally***: Allow yourself to feel your emotional state. Do you feel hurried or worried? Do you feel content or happy? Do you feel neutral? Are you in awe of the natural beauty around you? Do you long for more green space and natural surroundings? Do you feel inspired to incorporate more mindfulness into your life? Or do you feel this is a silly and nonsensical exercise? Allow yourself to recognize your emotions without judgment or trying to change them.
6. **Experience**: Now allow yourself to experience everything all at once, what you see, hear, smell, and feel. Relish that your body allows you to have such a complex sensory system and that you can experience so many things simultaneously.

If your mind drifts off and you start thinking of other things while doing this exercise, just gently remind yourself to redirect back to your intention of the walking meditation, which is to fully experience the present moment. Some days might be more difficult than others. If you feel particularly anxious or overwhelmed that day, you may find yourself redirecting your attention back several times over and over. That is absolutely fine. If you cannot leave your home, or if the weather does not permit, you can still do this while sitting on your couch or porch or walking inside your home or in your backyard.

The beauty of mindfulness and meditation is there is no "doing it wrong." Nobody is judging you, grading you, or even watching you.

Many caregivers find that fitting meditation into their day more than makes up for the time it takes. The divine feminine qualities—intuition, patience, wisdom, and love—often depend on how rested and free of stress we are and how aligned we are with what nourishes us.

After this small amount of time with which you have gifted yourself, you will become more clear, more mindful, and more grateful. The benefits are numerous and bountiful. Happy walking!

To download an audio version of this walking meditation, please visit:
https://spring-pond-99315.myflodesk.com/preorder-walking-meditation

Appendix C: Recommendations

For Parents

Books

100 Natural Remedies for Your Child, Jared Skowren, ND
Healing New Childhood Epidemics, Dr. Kenneth Bock
Healthy Kids, Happy Kids: An Integrative Pediatrician's Guide to Whole Child Resilience, Elisa Song, MD
How Doctors Think, Jerome Goopman, MD
Natural Baby and Childcare, Lauren Feder, MD
Treatment Alternatives for Children, Dr. Lawrence Rosen
Parenting at Your Child's Pace: The Integrative Pediatrician's Guide to the First Three Years of Life, Joel Warsh, MD

Websites

https://healthykidshappykids.com, by Dr. Elisa Song
https://www.bentonintegrative.com/healthtips, by Dr. Cammy Benton

Instagram

@drjoelgator
@drmariatemple
@wholistickids
@healthykids_happykids

For Healthcare Providers

All of the above plus:

Books

Better, Atul Gawande, MD
Between Heaven and Earth, Efrem Korngold and Harriet Beinfield
Integrative Pediatrics, Hilary McClafferty, MD
Love, Medicine, & Miracles, Bernie Siegel, MD
Mind Over Medicine, Lissa Rankin, MD
The Hidden Places, Ross Douthat
The Holistic Pediatrician, Kathy Kemper, MD
Why People don't Heal, and How They Can, Carolyn Myss, PhD
Wherever You Go, There You Are, Jon Kabat-Zinn

Programs

Andrew Weil Center for Integrative Medicine
https://integrativemedicine.arizona.edu

The Graduate Institute for Holistic Studies
https://learn.edu/integrative-health-and-healing/

The Institute for Functional Medicine
https://www.ifm.org/certification-membership/certification-program/

Websites

Holistic Primary Care
https://holisticprimarycare.net

Medical Academy of Pediatric Special Needs (MAPS)
https://www.medmaps.org

ACKNOWLEDGMENTS

To my mother and father, **Lynn and Tom**, thank you for all your love, guidance, and support. I am so lucky to have such incredible, smart, and interesting parents. Through your differences, I found a balance that has helped me become who I am today.

To my children, **Anna, Lilli,** and **Ava**, I have learned so much from each of you. I know you were mature and patient with me at times when I wish you never had to be. Just watching you grow into the incredible and beautiful women you are has been such an honor. My heart bursts with love and awe for each of you.

To my partner, **Lawrence Baril**, I appreciate your patience, calmness, and steadfastness more than you know. I couldn't have done it without you. You are my rock. You are my love.

To my dear friend and soul sister, **Martha Langer**, AKA GW, I can't thank you enough for all the "two-for-ones." I know I wouldn't be who I am today without you. Forever grateful.

To my *sister-from-another-mother*, **Alison Cargill**, AKA sweetpea, I cherish our friendship, our girl trips, our laughing so hard that we pee our pants moments, but most of all, our ability to be authentic, real, and raw.

To my business partner, **Dr. Molly DeMers**, I know it was divine intervention that brought us together in our mutual mission and desire to provide care in a better way. We have already been through much together in seven years. It is a wonder we haven't fallen apart! It is a great honor to grow with you.

To **Astara Jane Ashley**, my amazing mentor and publisher, who helped me FINALLY birth this book after many years of writing on and off, and get past my fears, blocks, procrastination, and self-doubt.

To all the amazing Rockstar integrative and holistic healthcare providers who have forged the path and led the way. Thank you for your bravery, brilliance, and ability to think outside the box. There are too many to name them all in fear of forgetting someone who deserves to be mentioned. I am forever honored and humbled by your service! But especially to my mentors, **Dr. Aviva Romm, Dr. Larry Rosen, and Dr. Elisa Song.**

I have never thought of myself as a Whitney Houston fan. But I do respect her artistry, vocal expression, and incredible voice. These words in "The Greatest Love of All" at the beginning of each chapter of this book have resonated with me since the first time I heard the song. So, I must give **Linda Creed** acclaim since she is the one who wrote it.

ABOUT THE AUTHOR

Lara O'Neil, APRN, CPNP

With over thirty years of experience working with children and families, Lara has worked in home care, hospitals, schools, and a primary care pediatric office. She currently owns a thriving integrative pediatric and family wellness center. She is an author, healer, and respected pediatric provider.

Lara is a Certified Pediatric Nurse Practitioner with a Master's in Arts from the College of St. Catherine in St. Paul, Minnesota. She holds additional certifications in Integrative Health and Healing, as well as Cranial Sacral Therapy and Reiki healing.

Yoga and meditation are integral to Lara's daily life, complemented by her love for biking, hiking, and the ocean. A passionate protector of innocence—animals, children, and the earth—she resides in Connecticut with her lifetime partner and two eccentric cats, taking immense pride in her three uniquely different and incredible daughters.

Explore more at **www.laraoneil.com**
and **www.thrivecenterforhealth.com**

FLOWER *of* LIFE PRESS

floweroflifepress.com

Made in the USA
Middletown, DE
28 October 2024